W0016855

Dancing with Colonels

NDSU

Dancing

with Colonels

A Young Woman's Adventures

in Wartime Turkey

Letters by MARJORIE HAVREBERG

Edited by JUDY BARRETT LITOFF

Compiled by SALLY ENSTROM

South Dakota

State Historical Society

Press Pierre

© 2011 by the South Dakota
State Historical Society Press
All rights reserved. This book
or portions thereof in any form
whatsoever may not be reproduced
without the expressed written approval
of the South Dakota State Historical
Society Press, 900 Governors Drive,
Pierre, S.Dak. 57501.

This publication is funded,
in part, by the Great Plains
Education Foundation, Inc.,
Aberdeen, S.Dak.

The paper in this book meets the
guidelines for permanence and durability
of the committee on Production
Guidelines for Book Longevity of the
Council on Library Resources.

Text and cover design by Rich Hendel

Please visit our website at
www.sdshspress.com

Printed in the United States of America

15 14 13 12 11   1 2 3 4 5

Library of Congress
Cataloging-in-Publication Data
Havreberg, Marjorie, 1914–1999.
Dancing with colonels : a young woman's
adventures in wartime Turkey : letters /
by Marjorie Havreberg ; edited by Judy
Barrett Litoff ; compiled by Sally Enstrom.
    p. cm.
Includes index.
ISBN 978-0-9845041-3-8 (alk. paper)
1. Havreberg, Marjorie, 1914–1999—
Correspondence. 2. World War,
1939–1945—Personal narratives, American.
3. World War, 1939–1945—Turkey—
Ankara. 4. Americans—Turkey—
Ankara—Correspondence.
5. Young women—Turkey—Ankara—
Correspondence. 6. Ankara (Turkey)—
Social life and customs—20th century.
7. Ankara (Turkey)—Biography. 8. World
War, 1939–1945—Washington (D.C.)
9. Washington (D.C.)—Social life and
customs—20th century. 10. Washington
(D.C.)—Biography. I. Litoff, Judy Barrett.
II. Enstrom, Sally, 1939– III. Title.
D811.5.H378 2011
940.53′561092—dc23

                                2011034295

Contents

Introduction
From Redfield to Washington to Ankara

BY JUDY BARRETT LITOFF

Marjorie Havreberg, known to her family and friends as Marge, grew up in the small town of Redfield, South Dakota, the county seat of Spink County. The first settlers had arrived in the area in 1878, adopting the "Redfield" name in 1881. As a railroad center served by the Chicago & North Western Railway and the Chicago, Milwaukee, Saint Paul & Pacific Railroad, also known as the Milwaukee Road, Redfield soon became a major town in northeastern South Dakota. However, its population has never exceeded three thousand. Like many of South Dakota's early citizens, Havreberg traced her roots to Scandinavia. Her Norwegian grandparents immigrated to the United States in the 1870s and eventually made their way to Dakota Territory, where they joined other Scandinavian immigrants who had come to the area with the hope of finding fertile land on which to establish homesteads. Her mother, Bessie Satter, was born in Carthage, a tiny town in northern South Dakota, in 1889, the year that South Dakota became a state. Her father, Henry Havreberg, born in 1874, eventually made his way to Carthage working as a well driller, and the couple married on 3 March 1910. Their first two children, Lillian (1911–1955) and Marjorie (1914–1999), were born in Carthage. Their third and last child, Patricia (1927–1996), was born after the family moved to Redfield, where Marjorie's father began working for Norbeck & Nicholson, a prosperous artesian well-drilling company headed up by Peter Norbeck, a highly successful businessman and South Dakota politician. It would be contact with Norbeck that prompted the young Marjorie Havreberg to shake the prairie dust from her shoes and travel the wide world.[1]

In 1920, the year that the Havrebergs moved to Redfield, Peter Norbeck was serving as the popular Republican governor of South Dakota, a position he had held since 1917. He was the state's first native-born governor. In the fall, Norbeck decided to run for the United States Senate, easily winning the election. He remained in that position until his death in 1936. He was a progressive Republican in the tradition of

Theodore Roosevelt and is credited with the inclusion of Roosevelt's image on the Mount Rushmore National Memorial. A conservationist who worked to protect the nation's natural resources, Norbeck's most prominent achievements in Congress were the passage of the 1928 Migratory Bird Act and the securing of funds needed to complete the Mount Rushmore project. He also supported legislation that established Grant Teton National Park in Wyoming and extended the boundaries of Yellowstone National Park. By the 1930s, Norbeck's progressivism found him increasingly at odds with the politics of the conservative wing of the Republican Party. In 1936, when Idaho Senator William E. Borah, the Progressive candidate for the Republican presidential nomination, lost his bid to Kansas governor Alf Landon, Norbeck broke ranks with his party and endorsed the re-election of Franklin D. Roosevelt.[2]

As Norbeck pursued his successful career in business and politics, Havreberg was enjoying a wholesome childhood in Redfield. She attended Redfield High School, where she met and became friends with a young teacher. Tom Jenkins had come from Oaks, North Dakota, in 1930 to teach industrial arts. He was six years older than Havreberg, but after she graduated from high school in 1932, their relationship grew serious. During Christmas 1933, they became engaged but made no definite wedding plans. Jenkins continued to teach at Redfield High School while pursuing a master's degree from Iowa State College. In 1934, after receiving his degree, he secured a teaching position in the department of industrial arts at Minot State Teacher's College (now Minot State University) in Minot, North Dakota. After she graduated from high school, Havreberg worked for the credit bureau in Redfield for a year. In the fall of 1933, she entered Nettleton Business College in Sioux Falls, South Dakota, where she studied stenography, bookkeeping, and typing. Drawing upon her newly acquired skills, she began working in May 1934 as a secretary for George Norbeck, the senator's brother, who now headed up the increasingly prosperous Norbeck artesian well-drilling company, headquartered in Redfield.[3] At the end of 1935, Havreberg was offered the opportunity to go to Washington, D.C., to work for a year as a clerical assistant for Julian Blount, Senator Peter Norbeck's private secretary. Prior to her leaving for the nation's capital in early January 1936, Havreberg and Jenkins broke off their engagement.

On 1 January 1936, twenty-one-year-old Marjorie Havreberg joined Senator and Mrs. Lydia Norbeck and several staff members for the long train ride to Washington. From the moment she arrived in the nation's capital, Havreberg embraced her new life. In her first letter to her mother, written on 5 January, she exclaimed: "I don't see how I am going to find time to write letters at all. I'm so happy about everything."[4] Over the next four months, Havreberg would experience an exhilarating world that contrasted sharply with small-town life in Redfield. Even though it was the height of the Great Depression, Washington was a bustling city, and Havreberg's letters provide little evidence of the poverty and turmoil that gripped much of the nation. She wrote of stopping by the Mayflower Hotel lobby, "the most luxurious place I have ever been in," eating raw oysters in the Senate dining room, and visiting the Library of Congress with its "elaborately decorated interior" and "beautiful" mosaic work. Although she was careful and sometimes even frugal in her spending, she seemed isolated from the worst throes of the depression.[5]

For most of her time in Washington, Havreberg lived at the Betty Alden Inn, a small boarding house for young working women, located at 125 B Street Southeast. The Betty Alden served home-style meals and provided a common room in which lodgers could gather at the end of the day to get to know each other and talk about their lives in the nation's capital. Her roommate, Gladys, whom she described in a letter to her mother as a "grand girl," taught music at a local junior high school. But most of the women at the Betty Alden had come to Washington to take advantage of the many government jobs that had been created as the federal bureaucracy expanded with the establishment of hundreds of New Deal agencies designed to combat the worst evils of the depression. These young women came from across the United States, and Havreberg remarked in one letter, "I don't believe there are two girls in this house from the same state."[6]

Upon arriving in Washington, Havreberg quickly developed a close circle of friends with whom she shared many adventures. During her early days there, she hardly wrote a letter in which she did not call attention to how much these friendships meant to her. Included in this close-knit group were Gladys, her roommate; Sally Norbeck, the senator's daughter; Josie, a co-worker at the Norbeck office; and several of the boarders at the Betty Alden, including Carrietta, Franky, and Mary. As time progressed, her circle of friends widened, and she remarked in a letter written to her sister Lillian in late March 1936, "One of the main reasons I like it here and I'm so happy is because I'm meeting new people all the time and haven't time to look back."[7]

Although she wrote at first that her prospects for dating were rather slim as "there are about ten girls to every boy in this town," casual dating, including white-tie affairs that sometimes kept her out until the wee hours of the morning, soon became a part of her routine.[8] She had arrived in Washington somewhat disconsolate about her failed engagement to Tom Jenkins, but by late March, she wrote: "I don't sound much like a broken-hearted girl . . . do I? I'm glad, of course." In early April, she reiterated: "I'm leading such a happy, carefree selfish life. I feel guilty. I haven't done anything to deserve it—I'm just lucky I guess."[9]

Havreberg worked at Norbeck's office, located in what is now known as the Russell Senate Office Building, from 9:00 A.M. to 6:00 P.M., with one hour off for lunch, each weekday. She occasionally returned to the office in the evening to complete unfinished projects or to type letters to her family back in South Dakota. She often had to work on Saturdays and Sundays, as well, but she never complained about the busy work schedule and still found time to take in the sights and sounds of Washington and its environs. Coming from South Dakota where the winters were long and harsh, she marveled at the warmth of Washington in January, noting, "the grass is green here you know and they have stands out doors on streets with cut flowers." She contrasted a warm spell in late February, which made it smell and look like spring, with the freezing weather her family was experiencing in South Dakota.[10]

Comments about major political events also made their way into Havreberg's letters. Following the 6 January 1936 United States Supreme Court decision that the processing taxes instituted under the Agricultural Adjustment Act of 1933 were unconstitutional, she reported that the decision "seems to be causing some excitement and a lot of uneasiness on the part of its 6,000 employees."[11] She wrote of attending a meeting of the Senate Munitions Committee that investigated reports that armament manufacturers had unduly influenced the United States to enter World War I and which, in turn, helped spark the adoption of neutrality legislation in the mid-1930s. She told of attending the swearing-in ceremony of Mrs. Huey Long, widow of the well-known Louisiana politician and United States senator who had been assassinated on 8 September 1935. She frequently attended Little Congress, an organization of stenographers and secretaries "on the Hill" who discussed and debated the questions that came up before the United States Congress.[12]

Having grown up in a small South Dakota town, Havreberg found much about life in metropolitan Washington both new and exciting. She wrote of attending a horse show at nearby Fort Myer, Virginia, with the entire Norbeck office staff, her awe at how fast short-order cooks at drugstore counters worked, her first ride on an "electric stairway" in a department store, enjoying numerous cocktail parties, celebrating her birthday at the famous Madrillon supper club, and playing the popular depression-era board game "Monopoly." She told her family of trips to movies, plays, art galleries, a chamber-music concert at the Library of Congress, and lectures by Carl Sandburg and other luminaries.[13] In no way did Havreberg's small-town upbringing impede her active social life. In fact, she seemed determined to take in as much of Washington as possible. She went to Constitution Hall to hear the famous Italian opera tenor Nino Martini sing, even though she admitted to her folks, "Everything I had read about him was so disgustingly conceited that I thought I wouldn't like it at all but I wanted to go because it is part of Washington that I want some of." To her utter surprise, she "thoroughly" enjoyed the concert.[14] Havreberg also heard Cornelia Otis Skinner perform at the National Theater and reported that the actress and author was "simply marvelous."[15] She regularly attended programs sponsored by the National Geographic Society and, of course, made certain to visit the major historical sites of Washington and its environs.

Senator Norbeck and his wife normally closed down their apartment at the fabled Kennedy-Warren complex, the Washington home of many wealthy congressmen and senators, in mid-May and returned to South Dakota for the summer. But a malignant throat cancer forced the senator to return to South Dakota in late March 1936. The Norbecks insisted that Havreberg come and live with Sally and her mother from 1 April until the anticipated mid-May closing of the Warren. Although Havreberg was reluctant to leave her friends at the Betty Alden Inn, she accepted this generous offer, remarking in a letter home: "I'm in the grandest bed I've ever slept in in my life. It's Mrs. Norbeck's. She has taken the Senator's room and Sally and I have this room with the twin beds in it."[16]

Not especially eager to return to life in small-town South Dakota, Havreberg began looking for other secretarial positions in Washington and arranged to take the civil-service examination. However, in late April, Senator Norbeck personally requested that she return to South Dakota to take care of his correspondence, and she readily complied. She remained with the ailing senator for the next eight months, both at the Mayo Clinic in Rochester, Minnesota, where he went for treatment, and in South Dakota. During the last months of Norbeck's life, she acted as both his nurse and secretary. She was at the senator's bedside in Redfield when he died on 20 December 1936.[17]

In January 1937, Havreberg moved to Pierre, the capital of South Dakota, to work as secretary to James E. Stewart, the state superintendent of banks. There she met her future husband, Paul Steinbach, who was also a state worker. They married in Redfield on 1 August 1937. The young couple eventually made their way back to Washington and, in February 1938, Havreberg was appointed junior stenographer in the office of the chief of finance of the War Department. Due to her excellent clerical skills, she received several promotions over the next four years. Her marriage to Steinbach, however, was not so successful. In August 1942, marital difficulties caused her to resign her position as the personal secretary of Colonel James B. Haley, acting chief of the administrative division in the office of finance. The couple was not able to resolve their marital problems; they separated in 1943 and divorced in May 1945.[18]

Following her resignation, Havreberg continued to work in Washington for the next two years. With World War II now raging, clerical workers were in high demand as legions of businessmen, academicians, "dollar a year" men, and other experts converged on the city to support the war effort. She held a part-time job as stenographer and secretary with the Department of State from August 1942 until March 1943. She was subsequently re-employed by the office of finance as a senior accounting clerk who assisted in auditing accounts at the national headquarters of the American Red Cross.[19]

During the summer of 1943, Havreberg began to explore the possibility of overseas service with either the Department of State or the Department of War. Part of her motivation for taking this momentous step was to assuage her disappointment over her failed marriage. The State Department application process was especially long and cumbersome. It consisted of gathering letters of recommendation from former and current government employers, a thorough medical examination, and an extensive background check that included interviews with many of Havreberg's friends, associates, and former employers. In a 1944 letter to her mother, she reported that Harold Norbeck, the senator's son, and Julian Blount had both written to let her know that they had been contacted by the State Department. But what really surprised Havreberg were the visits by State Department representatives to Redfield. In the same letter, she commented: "I have been scared ever since I found out that someone actually visited the home town for no other reason. It's just that it makes me nervous to have someone comb over my Past with a fine tooth comb and it makes me feel unduly important. They certainly go to great lengths for a piddling job."[20]

In early May, Havreberg learned that she had been accepted for overseas duty by both departments. After weighing the pros and cons of each, she chose the War Department because the State Department could not guarantee her a position for at least two or three months. The War Department, on the other hand, offered her a definite two-year position as a stenographer to the military attaché at the United States Embassy in Ankara, Turkey. A three-week training program at the newly constructed Pentagon was scheduled to begin on 16 May, followed by transport to Ankara where stenographers were in short supply. In a letter to her mother, Havreberg enthusiastically reported: "I'm getting ready to go to Turkey. Don't fall over in a faint now. I'm thrilled to pieces about it." In this long, typed, single-spaced, four-and-one-half-page letter, she provided her mother with detailed information about how she came to this decision, commenting: "For a while I sort of had cold feet on the whole deal and looked around at beautiful Washington—the trees and everything and thought of the comforts of living and the advantages that there are here and I confess I was frightened for a few minutes. But I also knew that I had very sincerely wanted to go overseas for too long to pass it up and that if I didn't I'm sure it would give me a complex for life that I was a coward and didn't care for anything except easy living." She concluded, "I don't feel that I'm showing a spark of courage either—I'm simply following the line of least resistance and selfishly doing what I want to do too."[21] The enthusiasm and excitement with which she had greeted the city as a young twenty-one-year-old fresh from Redfield in January 1936 had considerably diminished after eight years. The novelty of Washington, even a wartime Washington that was abuzz with life, had worn off. Thirty-year-old Havreberg, now wiser and more sophisticated, was looking for more out of life. Ankara, Turkey, seemed the perfect opportunity.

Over the course of the next month, Havreberg's life was a frenzy of packing up her apartment, shipping some goods back to Redfield and storing others at a nearby friend's house, completing her training course, reading as much as she could about Turkey, getting numerous immunizations, and purchasing a supply of clothes, toiletries, and other personal items that would sustain her during her two-year tour of duty. Her route to Ankara would be mostly by air, and she strategized about ways to stay within the seventy-seven-pound weight limit imposed by the airlines. The government agreed to ship additional baggage, totaling no more than four hundred pounds, but she could not count on these extras to arrive for at least six months.

With World War II raging, international travel could be dangerous, but Havreberg urged her parents to "please, please don't worry."[22] Following a phone call to her family on Father's Day, 18 June, in which her parents expressed their concerns about her forthcoming travels, she wrote, "It's wonderful to have someone who cares that much about you but worrying is so senseless & there will be no more danger for me than there is every day just in struggling with traffic and what not. . . . When I think of going, the trip, & being away for two years I'm excited, happy, and thrilled about it, but I know it's completely selfish—because I'm not sure that you feel that way."[23]

Ellen Clarkson, a twenty-three-year-old war widow and stenographer from Blackwood, New Jersey, would be heading to Ankara with Havreberg. By mid-June, both women were anxious to begin their journey. "Ellen and I get so discouraged," Havreberg wrote to her parents. "One day it seems that we'll be around for a couple of months and the next it seems we'll get our notice soon. At the moment it's the latter, but it's hard to know."[24] In fact, they departed the next day from Washington for Miami. After a nine-day layover in which they "nearly died of boredom," the two women continued their long journey via Puerto Rico, British Guiana, Brazil, Ghana, Egypt, and finally Turkey. Writing from Brazil on 4 July, Havreberg stated that she loved flying, "It's like being in another world." She saw "the Amazon River, jungles and more jungles, [and] . . . slept under mosquito netting."[25] In a subsequent letter, she added that she "watched a camel caravan go by" while in West Africa and queried: "Does it sound as strange to you as it does to me? To have seen the Amazon and the Nile, the pyramids, and had cocktails at Shepheard's in Cairo. I wish I really had the capacity to make the most of all this, but at any rate I enjoy it."[26] The entire trip took twenty-seven days, ending with her arrival in Turkey on 15 July. In her first letter to her family from Ankara, she remarked that she had "enjoyed" the trip but "got sort of tired of living out of a duffle bag."[27]

When Havreberg arrived in Turkey in July 1944, she entered a country that had skillfully managed to maintain its neutrality despite increasing pressure from both the Allied and Axis powers. At the outbreak of war in Europe in September 1939, the Republic of Turkey, founded in 1923, was a young, underdeveloped, and economically weak nation. President Ismet Inönü, who had succeeded the founder and first president of Turkey, Mustafa Kemal Atatürk, upon his death in November 1938, had been in office less than a year.[28] Inönü had personally experienced the hardships his country had suffered during World War I (1914–1918) with the defeat of the Ottoman Empire and the ensuing Turkish War of Independence (1919–1923), and he wanted to keep the young republic out of another war for which it was woefully unprepared. However, Turkey's strategic location as the gateway between Europe and the Middle East, its approaches to central Asia, its control of the Turkish Straits, and its access to the Black Sea meant that both the Allies and the Axis considered Turkey to be of strategic importance. Still, for most of the war, Turkey managed to maintain its neutrality. Not until 2 August 1944 did the country break off diplomatic relations with Germany, and it did not declare war against the Axis until 23 February 1945, a largely symbolic gesture and a necessary precondition for Turkey's participation in the United Nations Conference to be convened in San Francisco the following April.[29]

With the establishment of the Republic of Turkey on 29 October 1923, Mustafa Kemal had begun instituting a series of reforms designed to bring about a modern, democratic, secular state. These reforms included the movement of the capital from Istanbul to Ankara, located some two hundred twenty miles inland in central Anatolia. Ankara had served as the headquarters of the resistance movement during the Turkish War of Independence, and its population in 1923 was about twenty-five thousand. A British visitor to Ankara that year described it as "a tumble-down inferior Turkish town, of filthy streets and dirty, foul-smelling houses."[30] But over the course of the next two decades, Ankara experienced remarkable growth and development, and by 1944, its population had grown to about one hundred and ninety thousand. Ankara had two distinct parts: Ankara proper, which included the old city with winding streets and ancient buildings reflecting Roman, Byzantine, and Ottoman history; and the new section, called Yenisehir, with wide avenues and boulevards lined with shade trees and flower gardens where government offices and foreign embassies were located. By the 1940s, Ankara was well on its way to becoming a modern city. Sidewalk cafés abounded, and, according to a May 1945 *National Geographic* article, "pretty young Turkish girls, short of skirt, sheer of stocking, and red of lip, [moved] with freedom and poise."[31] The American Embassy staff in Ankara concurred, reporting in 1945, "Today's visitor who sees the fine streets, large public buildings, greenness of planting and mildness of Ankara climate will marvel at the Turkish accomplishment in creating in 22 years such an attractive city."[32]

As the capital of a neutral country, Ankara welcomed representatives from both Allied and Axis countries. Social gatherings and receptions, of which there were many, required special planning. At the president's reception on Turkey's National Day each 29 October, planners relegated Allied guests to one room and Axis guests to another. Neutrals shuttled back and forth. At popular restaurants such as Karpiç's (also Karpitch's), a favorite of Havreberg's, owners such as the legendary Baba Karpiç skillfully navigated seating arrangements to ensure that Allied and Axis clients were seated far from each other. The *Saturday Evening Post* reported in May 1944 that Karpiç "studiously charted the dining room: northeast corner for Axis parties, southeast for satellites, and the remainder for Turks and Allies," while the center table was "sacrosanct" and always reserved for Prime Minister Numan Menemencioğlu.[33]

Like other neutral countries, Turkey was an intelligence battlefield where spies and counterspies abounded. Elyesa Banza, codenamed "Cicero," was the valet to the British ambassador to Turkey, Hughe Montgomery Knatchbull-Hugessen. By reading and photographing Knatchbull-Hugessen's mail, Banza was able to sell important Allied information to the Germans about international conferences and bombing raids, but the Germans did not usually act upon his information because they questioned its reliability. British intelligence considered Istanbul to be a crucial base for their Balkan operations. America's chief wartime intelligence agency, the Office of Strategic Services, also gathered important classified information on Germany and Nazi-occupied Europe from its operations in Turkey.[34]

As a stenographer and secretary in the office of Brigadier-General Richard Gentry Tindall, the United States Army military attaché in Ankara from 1943 to 1945, Havreberg must have been aware of these diplomatic intrigues, but her letters contain little to suggest that she knew anything about spies and counterspies. Years later, when preparing handwritten notes for a talk that she would present at an Elderhostel program about her experiences in Turkey, she acknowledged, "In wartime Ankara it was wisest to assume that everyone was an agent for one of the powers & those who weren't reporting to a foreign country you could be sure reported to the Turkish Secret Police who were suspicious of all foreigners & very thorough."[35]

During World War II, army military attachés were directly accountable to the War Department. In an era before satellite photography and sophisticated electronic intelligence-gathering techniques, they "were the Army's eyes and ears abroad" and "used overt means and sources to collect facts about foreign weapons specifications, military doctrine, and order of battle." They also advised the ambassador and his staff on military matters that affected the national interests of the United States. Technically, the ambassador was the attaché's commanding officer.[36]

General Tindall reported to Ambassador Laurence A. Steinhardt, who had arrived in Ankara to take up his post on 3 March 1942. For the previous three years, Steinhardt had served as ambassador to the Soviet Union during the critical period of German-Soviet détente, followed by the German invasion of the Soviet Union in June 1941. Steinhardt's reports on the political and economic situation in the Soviet Union were highly respected within the State Department, and "his appointment to the sensitive post in Ankara was an indication of his ability and reputation." Throughout his tenure in Ankara, Steinhardt urged the Allies to be patient and tolerant with Turkey, arguing that the Turks "should not be forced into the war against their will." In the summer of 1943, he reported to Washington, "There is much to be said for the Turkish point of view and . . . if the Turks are willing to go along at the right time, it would seem wiser to wait for the right time before pinpricking the Turks." Largely due to Steinhardt's moderate and measured approach, America's relations with Turkey remained cordial throughout the war years and helped to establish the framework for an even closer relationship between the two countries in the immediate postwar era. Given Turkey's strategic location, a strong alliance became even more crucial during the Cold War era as hostilities between the Soviet Union and the United States intensified.[37]

Havreberg's letters contain only brief passages about the actual work that she performed for General Tindall and his staff. She did write home that she had "at last found office hours that suit me fine—go to work at 9:30, have lunch from 1:30 to 3:00, and quit at 7 o'clock and we never go out to dinner till 9 o'clock."[38] The *Saturday Evening Post* quipped that a long lunch break was needed because it was "impossible to recover from Karpiç's screw drivers and steaks in less than three hours."[39] In a 29 September letter, Havreberg confided, "I like my work & the fellow I work with is very difficult, but I think he's beginning to believe I'm all right."[40] Less than three weeks later, she reported, "I love my work now and it's easy for me—the General told me the other day that I do the work of two WAC [Women's Army Corps] secretaries that he had before."[41] General Tindall was evidently quite pleased with Havreberg's work, for the following June he appointed her his private secretary. "The job is no joke," she told her family. "He works very much like the Senator did—and I'm enjoying it but it keeps me on my toes."[42] Although Havreberg's letters provide only limited descriptions of her stenographic and secretarial duties, she did make a special point to assure her family that she did, indeed, work, writing in one letter, "I do work too, you know—even though I talk about everything else but work."[43]

What Havreberg talked about most in her letters was her enthusiasm for her new life in Ankara, the excitement of being a part of a vibrant international community, the many friends, especially male friends, whom she had met, and Sunday excursions to the countryside that included picnics, hiking, and friendly exchanges with Turkish peasants. In a 26 August 1944 letter to her family, she exclaimed: "I think you remember how happy I was in Washington when I worked for the Senator. Have talked about that ever since but this has displaced it many times over. I have never had such fun, nor felt so good—both well and happy."[44] Of course, she recognized that not everyone shared her enthusiasm for Ankara, noting, "Europeans think it is awful, but I think it is interesting."[45] She looked forward to visiting Istanbul, but she decried the practice of government officials and foreign diplomats who left Ankara for Istanbul in the summer to escape the heat, arguing that this is "the most delightful climate I've ever known and why anyone leaves Ankara to go to Istanbul for the summer—I cannot understand."[46] Acknowledging in early September that perhaps she "looked at everything through rose-colored glasses," she proceeded in her next letter, dated 7 September, to discuss the inconveniences of living in Ankara. They included the cutting-off of water for large chunks of time each day, the incessant bedbug problem, sand flies, blackouts, and the language barrier. But her fondness for Ankara still came through as she concluded, "The truth is I never think of the things that are unpleasant—except when I'm forced to—like bedbugs for instance—they can be quite forceful."[47]

The letters contain vivid descriptions of Havreberg's great excitement at attending receptions and parties hosted by the British, Polish, and American embassies, as well as other foreign delegations. After attending "a long dress" party hosted by one of the secretaries of Ambassador Steinhardt, she reported, "There was a mixture of everyone—all nationalities—and I love parties like that."[48] Thanksgiving and Christmas included lively celebrations, replete with traditional American food, at Steinhardt's home. The Christmas Eve 1944 celebration at the ambassador's residence was done "up on a grand and generous scale," Havreberg reported, and much to her surprise, she danced with the ambassador.[49]

Havreberg also wrote fondly of dining and dancing at Karpiç's, remarking that its orchestra was "exceptionally good" and the garden at night is "one of the loveliest spots I've . . . ever been in—Ankara would be a cold and dismal place without it and sweet Baba Karpiç is the very heart of it."[50] By mid-October, her social life had become so crowded that she promised that she "was going to stay home every night for two weeks," but with so many opportunities coming her way, she immediately realized the futility of such a pledge.[51] For her thirty-first birthday, 12 March 1945, she informed her mother: "Had six men on my hands and was toasted so many times, and so many compliments— I know it made me giddy. . . . It's really too much, Mother—it's like living a charmed life since I've been here and one day I expect a terrific blow and I will come down to earth again."[52]

One reason for Havreberg's busy social life was the imbalance in the male/female ratio in Ankara. There were only "about 20 American girls here in Ankara," and "most parties have about two men for every girl," she recorded.[53] Of equal importance was Havreberg's exuberance for life and her willingness to take advantage of the many novel opportunities that Ankara had to offer. Men flocked to the side of this young, adventurous, and attractive woman, and her social life consisted of a whirlwind of dinners, parties, and receptions.[54] Havreberg cherished her growing circle of international friends, especially the many men she could now count among her acquaintances. In late August 1944, she remarked, "I have never lacked for friends among girls but I've never had men friends like this before and I think it's good for me."[55]

Among her favorite male acquaintances were three representatives of the Polish government-in-exile, which had been established after the German invasion of Poland on 1 September 1939 and eventually headquartered in London. Its men in Turkey included Colonel Marian Zimnal, the Polish military attaché; Colonel Jan Rudnicki, the assistant military attaché; and Antoni ("Balo") Balinski, counselor to the Polish Embassy. "I've met a great many people," Havreberg told her family in August 1944. "My favorites are three Poles and I love them. They are the most hospitable people and I always have a marvelous time with them. . . . They are all very good dancers—but with Antoni I could dance forever. . . . I have never cared much for dancing and I know that I couldn't before—but here it seems to be a new discovery for me and I love it."[56] Monday night soon became a regular date night for Havreberg and Balinski, and their friendship eased into romance. In a 21 February 1945 letter, she admitted, "Even though I go out with others and have fun and love being here—I dread to think of what it will be like if Balo should leave. We recently celebrated our 25th anniversary—25 Monday nights and there have been countless others in between. He is marvelous. . . . He's the kindest and most unselfish person I know."[57] Other men who figured prominently in Havreberg's life included Colonel Theodore Babbitt and Captain Walter Ewart Seager, both assistants to the United States military attaché; Jeffrey Short, a State Department employee who worked in the Office of the Counselor for Economic Affairs; Charles Lucet, first secretary at the French Embassy; and Major Peter Wainwright from England. As much as she enjoyed their company, however, it was her three Polish friends, most importantly Balinski, who remained dearest to her heart.

When Havreberg first arrived in Ankara in July 1944, she and Ellen Clarkson were housed at the Park Palas Hotel. After Clarkson, who did not share Havreberg's exuberance for Turkey, resigned her position and returned to the United States in November 1944, Havreberg rented a room in a nearby home for about six weeks. In mid-January 1945, she and co-worker Corelli Jernigan began sharing the first floor of a house with another co-worker, Barbara Turner. Three wood stoves provided heat for their apartment, and, according to Havreberg, "It's been very comfortable," but she emphasized, "what is more important than central heating is a hot water heater and we have that so we have hot showers or baths whenever we want them." They also had a Greek servant, Sultana, who did "everything" for them.[58] Havreberg and Jernigan continued this living arrangement until Havreberg's departure for the United States in mid-May 1946.

Havreberg wrote with awe about her frequent Sunday excursions to the Turkish countryside with her Polish and other friends. In an October 1944 letter, she reported, "In Ankara you could almost imagine you were in a town in the States . . . but as soon as you get into the country it's completely different." She told of driving in a jeep to a small village at the foot of a mountain the group intended to climb. Along the way, they observed peasants who wore "baggy trousers—generally patched till you can't tell what the original material was." She also noted, "The veil is supposed to be taboo, but not all the women in the country have discarded them." She described the peasants as "friendly and pleasant," and at one village where they stopped, the villagers insisted on plying them with delicious, freshly harvested grapes. In this same village, they saw women pressing grapes with their bare feet. When the group reached their final destination, they hired a donkey to carry their food and extra clothing to the top of the mountain, where the view was "marvelous" with "miles & miles of hills & mountains." For Havreberg, the highlight of the trip occurred when the muezzin came out on the flat rooftop of one of the huts in the village below to call the people to prayer. "That chant always fascinates me," she wrote. "I love it!"[59]

Without question, Havreberg's favorite trip to the country occurred on 31 December 1944, when she and seven of her friends, representing five nationalities, headed by jeep through the snow-covered countryside for an outdoor picnic to celebrate the last day of the year. When the party arrived at their destination, they realized that they were too wet and cold to eat outside. They then approached a small Turkish village of about one hundred fifty people and asked if they could come into someone's home to warm up and have their lunch. They were immediately invited into a "charming" room whose benches and floor were covered with Turkish rugs, and in the center of the room was a small stove. As they sat cross-legged on the floor, the room filled with curious villagers. Women, many of whom were veiled, scurried about, and it soon became clear that they were preparing food for their foreign guests. After a "quick consultation," the group agreed: "There was only one thing to do, we must eat their food and give them ours." The meal included flat breads that also served as napkins and large bowls of chicken and fish placed in the center of the table from which "everyone dipped." Havreberg commented, "I'm sure they must have thought our manners awful, but they seemed to enjoy the visit and they were certainly hospitable." From this extraordinary experience, the group then rushed back to Ankara for eggnog at a friend's house and then to a white-tie affair at the Czechoslovakian Embassy, which Havreberg described as "the biggest event of the season. All the diplomats were there and the crowd really glittered." A post-embassy party at another friend's house followed, and Havreberg reported that she did not get home until seven in the morning. She concluded, "It was a wonderful way to spend the last day of 44 and the first part of 45. Sunday morning to Monday morning seemed at least a week long it was so full."[60]

In late January 1945, Havreberg and Jernigan spent a memorable week visiting Jerusalem, Tel Aviv, Beirut, and Damascus. In a 5 February letter to her family, Havreberg remarked, "I'm sure it's a beautiful country at any time but coming from the snow and barrenness of Turkey we appreciated it all the more."[61] They also made three trips to Istanbul. After the first trip, a brief weekend visit in mid-August 1945, Havreberg wrote, "Istanbul is fantastic—the beauties of the Bosporus are impossible to describe, but Ankara is home to me and I prefer being here."[62] They returned to Istanbul in early September for a "perfectly marvelous vacation" of nearly two weeks.[63] They made a third and final trip to Istanbul in early April 1946 to visit the USS *Missouri,* the battleship that would serve as the site of the formal surrender of Japan on 2 September 1945. The *Missouri* was anchored in the Bosporus from 5 to 9 April 1946 to deliver the remains of Münir Ertegün, the Turkish ambassador to the United States, who had died in Washington in November 1944. Because the Turkish government had recently rejected the Soviet Union's demand for joint control of the Dardanelles and Bosporus Straits connecting the Mediterranean Sea to the Black Sea, the Turks were elated with this gesture of friendship by the United States at this particular time. "The Turks have been terrible impressed by the visit," Havreberg reported. "They have issued special *Missouri* stamps, *Missouri* cigarettes and stuff." She also recounted that they "stood on The Spot where the peace was signed" and attended a round of diplomatic dinners and parties that lasted until late at night.[64]

Havreberg's letters were silent on the topic of her estrangement from Paul Steinbach and their impending divorce. Only indirect references, such as how "deeply grateful" she was for the change in her life and "how differently" she now felt, provide hints about her failed marriage.[65] On another occasion, she wrote: "I suppose you think it's crazy all this going around but I love it and I know it's good for me. I never go to any of these things without expecting to enjoy them. . . . I don't have that old dread and feeling of shyness that I used to have."[66] Even so, she was known as Mrs. Marjorie Steinbach, and after one diplomatic party, she noted, "Had my hand kissed every time I turned around but I'm getting quite accustomed to it—that's what I get for having a 'Mrs.' in front of my name."[67] Given the imbalance in the male/female ratio among the foreign community in Ankara, including many married men whose wives did not join them, one's marital status did not take on the same importance as in the United States. Consequently, married and single persons mingled freely in a variety of social settings.

For the most part, commentary about the great events of the day did not make their way into Havreberg's letters, and political discussions were not her main focus. However, she assured her mother, "As far as being aware of the war—I may not write about it but I certainly am very conscious of it."[68] Havreberg usually commented only when events had a personal or special meaning for her. For example, after the liberation of Paris on 25 August 1944, she wrote of attending a gala party at the French Embassy to celebrate the exile of the Vichy French from the premises and their replacement by "our friends."[69] She alluded to the sixty-three-day Warsaw Uprising to liberate the city from Nazi occupation that ended in tragic failure on 2 October 1944 when she wrote her mother that she had not danced with Balo for almost two weeks because the Poles were "observing a period of mourning for those who were killed in Warsaw."[70] She recorded her great excitement at being invited to General Tindall's home to listen to a special radio broadcast about the 7 November 1944 election when President Franklin D. Roosevelt was elected to an unprecedented fourth term. She exclaimed: "I got a thrill out of hearing the announcer say, in describing the momentous evening so important and of such interest to the entire world, that the American Ambassador was at General Tindall's house with other friends listening to the radio and I thought gosh—I'm here too. That's us!"[71] Five months later, following the death of President Roosevelt on 12 April 1945, she described a memorial service at the American Embassy: "All the diplomats were there in uniform as morning suits. My Poles looked nice. Marian (Col. Zimnal) in uniform with his shoulder weighted down with a whole lot of medals. Balo in top hat, cutaway coat, and striped trousers. . . . Still my favorite people in Ankara."[72]

A month-long period of mourning followed the death of Roosevelt, which meant that there could be no official celebrations at the American Embassy to mark the end of the war in Europe on 8 May 1945. In a 10 May letter, Havreberg remarked that it had been a bit "awkward," and while the Americans were not celebrating, the British "have been both officially and privately and the Russians put a big sign on the Embassy with the word 'Victory' (in Russian of course) in blue lights and they celebrated all night." Reflecting the feelings of many citizens of the United States, she continued, "Of course, it's good that poor old tired Europe can rest and recuperate and I'm happy that it's over but couldn't feel very elated about the news—suppose it's because the war in the Pacific is still going on."[73]

With the dropping of the atomic bombs on Hiroshima and Nagasaki on 6 and 9 August, Havreberg waited anxiously for news that the war had finally ended. On 14 August 1945, she exclaimed: "Aren't the atomic bombs the most fantastic thing—sounds like something out of Buck Rogers' comic strip. Everyone's been talking about them." When the news of peace overtures reached them, she continued: "The office was fun all afternoon and the General quickly arranged a cocktail party for that night. We went to that and afterwards to Karpitch's for dinner and every last American was there that night I guess. We are hoping each day to hear that the fighting has stopped and that the war is really over."[74] The announcement of Japan's surrender occurred on Wednesday, 15 August. The formal surrender took place aboard the USS *Missouri* docked in Tokyo Bay on 2 September 1945.

In mid-August, Havreberg proffered the news that Turkey had recognized the newly-established, Communist-controlled Polish government in Warsaw. All of her Polish friends were representatives of the London-based anti-Communist Polish government-in-exile and therefore must leave Turkey. As Allied powers withdrew their support for the government-in-exile during the summer of 1945, the Poles based in London were forced to vacate their embassy and seek out private residencies. Many Poles in exile, including those who had fought for the Allies, were unwilling to return to Communist Poland for fear of persecution and sought refuge in other countries, such as Great Britain and the United States. Although largely unrecognized and without effective power, representatives of the Polish government-in-exile remained in London until December 1990 when Lech Walesa became the country's first post-Communist president.[75]

During the summer of 1945, with the future of the Polish government-in-exile in doubt, Balo applied for an American immigration visa. He received it in October and left Ankara later that month, arriving in the United States in late November. As Balinski prepared to leave, he showered Havreberg with gifts. In a 24 October letter to her mother, Havreberg wrote: "Everyone tells us how attractive our house is now and of course we know Balo deserves all the credit. It's full of things from him—vases, pictures, flowers, etc., etc. Besides I have countless personal gifts from him—bracelets, ear rings, silver cups, and doo dads. And I'll never part with any of his gifts. Guess I'll have a bag full of those things along when I come home."[76] In a 25 October "congratulations" letter to her eighteen-year-old sister Pat, who had recently married George ("Du") DuChateau, a young enlisted man in the navy, Havreberg confided, "My Balo is leaving on Monday by boat for the States and I'm going to miss him very much."[77]

With Balinski gone and many of her other friends receiving new assignments or returning to their home countries, Havreberg's thoughts turned increasingly to her family in South Dakota. In a 16 December 1945 letter to her mother, she remarked, "Glad I have only a few months to go—the place is getting too full of memories for me—like a ghost town."[78] But in a subsequent letter, written three weeks later, she admitted that Christmas and New Years had been "lots of fun." New Years Eve "was probably the most interesting," she wrote, as it involved small and large parties with many diplomats and Turkish government officials, including Prime Minister Şükrü Saracoğlu, with whom she shared a table for about thirty minutes. Just as on the previous New Years Eve, she partied through the night, returning home around 7:00 A.M.[79]

Nonetheless, as she contemplated returning to the United States, Havreberg's letters took on a more somber tone. She especially worried about the health of her mother, who in early January 1946 underwent surgery for colon cancer. "I do want to see all of you very much," Havreberg wrote on 10 February 1946, "and I think it's necessary to come home to be re-Americanized, but I like foreign service so much that if it were not for Balo—I'm sure I'd stay over another year. Then, I would get home leave with transportation home." Twelve days later, she wrote her mother, "I have decided definitely to leave in May and I am literally counting the days." In early March, she reiterated, "Gosh, I'm getting so anxious to be on my homeward way I'm practically fliberty giberty—whatever that is, but it sounds like me." With millions of war-weary servicemen waiting for transport back to the United States, she wondered how long it would take her to get home. "They say," she added, "that at the moment there is such a backlog in Paris and even worse in England that one may be held up weeks at either place."[80]

On 18 April 1946, Havreberg received orders from the office of the military attaché to proceed to the United Sates on or about 15 May. In a letter to her mother, she exclaimed: "Only 26 days and I'll be on my way. . . . Am so excited about leaving. . . . Have loved it here—it has been wonderful. . . . But now I'm terribly thrilled to realize that I'll be home again so soon."[81] Havreberg's trip home began on 16 May when she flew from Ankara to Cairo. The fascination with which she had greeted Cairo on her way to Ankara in July 1944 had dissipated, and she now found the city to be "horrible" with "intense heat, filth, and flies." She did, however, enjoy a return visit to Shepheard's and remarked: "It's true what they say about Shepheard's terrace—if you sit there long enough you'll see the whole world pass by. The first evening there, saw at least ten people I knew." Her next flight took her to England, where she confided to her family: "It was hard to leave Turkey. Guess I still have lots of friends there. There were parties, luncheons, cocktail and dinner every day the last week. . . . Lots of people were at the airport. . . . After they said it was time to get on the plane, it took another ten minutes to kiss everyone goodbye and Corelli cried, bless her heart. I didn't—I felt sort of sick."[82]

On 28 May, Havreberg set sail from Southampton for the United States on a transport ship, the USS *Holbrook,* and arrived in New York

City a week later. The *Holbrook* was one of several ships that transported some seventy-thousand British war brides and their babies to the United States to be reunited with their GI husbands and fathers. Alluding to widespread newspaper coverage about nine babies who had died from a mysterious illness during an April 1946 voyage on the *Holbrook*, Havreberg wrote, "I'm . . . expecting it may be pretty awful if the stories about these brides and babies are true." But the prospects of traveling with ailing babies and their anxious mothers could not dampen her enthusiasm for what she had experienced in Ankara. In her last letter home, she reiterated: "The two years were pretty wonderful and thank goodness I realized it while I was there. So many don't appreciate it till they leave. . . . I hope . . . there are other Ankaras ahead for me."[83]

The exigencies of World War II had provided Marjorie Havreberg with the extraordinary opportunity to travel to distant Ankara, Turkey, and experience the complexities and challenges of life in a neutral country of strategic importance to both the Allied and the Axis powers. There, she was part of an international circle of diplomats and civil servants who joined together in a variety of social and political settings, and this young and spirited woman took good advantage of all that Turkey had to offer. Her adventures in the Turkish countryside, at the formal affairs hosted by various embassies, and in dining and dancing at Karpiç's opened up new and unimaginable worlds to her. She celebrated the exile of the Vichy French from Ankara, mourned the tragic failure of the Warsaw Uprising, and, at the end of the war, agonized over Allied recognition of the Communist-controlled government in Poland. Indeed, she had a firsthand understanding of the complicated politics of World War II.

Havreberg's adventures can be experienced firsthand in the approximately one hundred sixty letters, both typed and handwritten, that she wrote to her family and close friends in 1936 from Washington, D.C., and in 1944–1946 from Ankara, Turkey. They are part of the Marjorie Havreberg Steinbach Jenkins Papers located in the State Archives Collection at the South Dakota State Historical Society in Pierre, the gift of her niece, Sally Enstrom, who collected and preserved them. Enstrom also compiled the letters for this publication and provided much detail on family background. In order to enhance the readability of the letters, occasional spelling and grammatical errors have been silently corrected. Ellipses indicate omissions. Explanatory endnotes provide historical context and identify key persons, places, and events.

Throughout the editing, the immediacy of these letters has been maintained. Once Havreberg begins working in the military attaché's office, she dates her letters in military style. This change is retained to reflect her new living and working environment. In the handwritten letters, Havreberg used dashes as well as periods between sentences. Through context and capitalization, the editor has attempted to determine when Havreberg intended to end a sentence and when she was adding an aside. Full of enthusiasm for her topics, Havreberg often had long paragraphs in her letters. These paragraphs have been broken into smaller units to enhance readability. Overall, however, Havreberg's prose—her long breathless sentences—have been left as she wrote them to allow readers to sense the excitement and frenetic pace of life in Washington, D.C., and then Ankara in wartime.

NOTES

1. Leta Ann Nolan, *History of the Spink County Area: In Celebration of South Dakota's Centennial, 1889–1989* (Dallas, Tex.: Curtis Media Corp., 1989), pp. 8–10, 39–50. Marjorie Havreberg would marry twice in her life, briefly in 1942 to Paul Steinbach and again in 1950 to Thomas Jenkins. For convenience and simplicity, her maiden name is used throughout this book, even though she went by the formal title of Mrs. Steinbach during her time in Turkey. For more information on the Havreberg family, I am indebted to Sally Enstrom, who compiled these letters and gave them to the South Dakota State Historical Society (SDSHS) in Pierre, where they are held as the Marjorie Havreberg Steinbach Jenkins Papers in the State Archives Collection.

2. The most comprehensive study of Peter Norbeck is Gilbert Courtland Fite, *Peter Norbeck: Prairie Statesman* (Pierre: South Dakota State Historical Society Press, 2005). *See also* O. W. Coursey, *Who's Who in South Dakota*, Vol. 3 (Mitchell, S.Dak.: Educator Supply Co., 1920), pp. 228–44.

3. According to Gilbert Fite, "Disagreement between Norbeck and Nicholson led to dissolution of their company [in 1924]. . . . Norbeck bought most of the equipment and incorporated the Norbeck Company, which was operated by his brother, George, as the old Norbeck and Nicholson had been since 1912" (Fite, *Peter Norbeck*, p. 115).

4. "Dear Mother," 5 Jan. 1936. All Havreberg letters can be found in the Jenkins Papers at SDSHS.

5. "Hello sweethearts," 5 Jan. 1936; "Dear Mother," 8 Jan. 1936.

6. "Dear Mother," 5, 8 Jan. 1936. For information on the New Deal agencies, *see* Herbert S. Schell, *History of South Dakota*, 4th ed., rev. John E. Miller (Pierre: South Dakota State Historical Society Press, 2004), pp. 288–95.

7. "Dearest Lillian," 22 Mar. 1936.

8. "Dear sweet Mother," 26 Feb. 1936. *See also* "Dear Lillian," 3, 4 Apr. 1936.

9. "Dearest Mother," 30 Mar. 1936; "Dearest Lillian," 6 Apr. 1936.

10. "Hello sweethearts," 5 Jan. 1936; "Dear sweet Mother," 26 Feb. 1936.

11. "Dear Dad," 7 Jan. 1936. The Agricultural Adjustment Act, enacted on 12 May 1933, restricted agricultural production by paying farmers to reduce crop acreage. A tax on companies who processed farm products generated the money for these subsidies. The Supreme Court ruled that the AAA was unconstitutional in levying this tax. Schell, *History of South Dakota*, pp. 288–90.

12. "Dear Dad," 7 Jan. 1936; "Dearest Mother," 9 Jan. 1936; "Dearest Lillian," 22 Feb. 1936.

13. "Dear Mother," 19 Jan. 1936; "Dear Lillian," 22 Jan. 1936; "Dear sweet Mother," 26 Feb. 1936; "Dearests," 16 Mar. 1936.

14. "Dear Folks," 20 Feb. 1936.

15. "Dearest Lillian," n.d. (most likely late Jan. 1936).

16. "Dearest Lillian," 3 Apr. 1936.

17. "Dearest Mother," 22 Apr. 1936; Fite, *Peter Norbeck*, pp. 201–5.

18. Little is known about the Steinbach marriage. Havreberg's sister and brother-in-law, Lillian and Floyd ("Duke") Enstrom, acted as witnesses to the ceremony. From 1938 to 1942, the couple lived in Washington, D.C., where they both held government jobs. In 1939, when Havreberg's niece Sally Enstrom was born, the Steinbachs were named the godparents. A 1948 resume included in the Jenkins Papers at SDSHS states that Marge resigned from her full-time job in August 1942 for "domestic reasons." By the summer of 1943, when Havreberg applied for overseas work, the couple had separated. A 14 August 1943 letter of recommendation written by Colonel James B. Haley stated: "She [Havreberg] left this office by resignation for personal reasons in August 1942 and was subsequently re-employed in February 1943 upon the termination of the circumstances which had required her absence. I am glad to recommend her for any position requiring responsible and careful work." Unfortunately, any letters that Havreberg may have written to her family during this period do not survive. The next letters begin in March 1944. At that time, Havreberg lived in a small apartment in Washington that she shared with a roommate and worked for the War Department. In a 7 April 1944 letter to her younger sister Patricia, she mentioned that she had gone to see the 1943 movie *The Song of Bernadette* with Paul and learned that he had a new job doing legal work for the joint committee of the National Association of Manufacturers and the United States Chamber of Commerce. She wrote: "I admit I had to swallow a couple of times, but I do sincerely think it's swell and I'm very happy for him. The boy is doing all right and I wish him luck." The divorce decree was filed on 1 May 1945 in Pierre by Havreberg's attorneys, Marten & Goldsmith. By this time, she was working in Ankara, Turkey. Steinbach was not present at the filing and did not contest the divorce.

19. Havreberg (Steinbach) Resume, Jenkins Papers. On life in Washington during World War II, *see* David Brinkley, *Washington Goes to War* (New York: Alfred A. Knopf, 1988). Businessmen who came to Washington to run various federal agencies often remained on their company's payroll and were paid one dollar a year by the United States government, becoming known as dollar-a-year men. Allan M. Winkler, "The World War II Home Front," *History Now,* www.gilderlehrman.org/history now/12_2007/historian3.php.

20. "Dearest Mother," [30] Apr. 1944.

21. "Dearest Mother," 14 May 1944.

22. "Dear Mother," [17] June 1944.

23. "Dear Mother," [18 June 1944].

24. Ibid.

25. "Dear Lillian," [25 June 1944]; "Dear Family," 4 July 1944.

26. "Dear Lillian," 14 Aug. 1944. Shepheard's was a rendezvous point for politicians, military officers, and spies during World War II.

27. "Dearest Family," 19 July 1944.

28. In 1934, Mustafa Kemal was awarded the title "Atatürk," meaning "father of the Turks," by the Turkish Grand National Assembly. Barry Rubin, *Istanbul Intrigues* (New York: Pharos Books, 1992), pp. 20–21.

29. David J. Alvarez, "The Embassy of Laurence A. Steinhardt: Aspects of Allied-Turkish Relations, 1941–1945," *East European Quarterly* 9 (1975): 39; Igor Lukes, "Ambassador Laurence Steinhardt: From New York to Prague," *Diplomacy and Statecraft* 17(2006): 533–39. In October 1939, one month after the outbreak of war in Europe, Turkey signed a treaty of mutual assistance with Great Britain and France. A Turkish-German treaty of friendship and non-aggression was signed on 18 June 1941, just four days before the German attack on the Soviet Union. Rubin, *Istanbul Intrigues*, pp. 38–39, 88. For a thorough discussion of Turkish foreign policy during World War II, *see* Selim Deringil, *Turkish Foreign Policy during the Second World War: An "Active Neutrality"* (Cambridge: Cambridge University Press, 1989).

30. Quoted in American Embassy, Ankara, "Information about Ankara for Transient Americans," 25 May 1945, p. 4, Jenkins Papers.

31. Maynard Owen Williams, "The Turkish Republic Comes of Age," *National Geographic* 87 (May 1945): 581. This article also included twenty-four full-page photographs.

32. "Information about Ankara," p. 4.

33. George Moorad, "Baba Walks a Tightrope," *Saturday Evening Post* 216 (13 May 1944): 6.

34. On intelligence gathering in Turkey during World War II, *see* Rubin, *Istanbul Intrigues*.

35. [Havreberg], handwritten notes, n.d., Jenkins Papers.

36. "The Role of US Army Military Attachés between the World Wars," https://www.cia.gov/library/center-for-the-study-of-intelligence/csi-publications/csi-studies/studies/95unclass/Koch.html.

37. Alvarez, "Embassy of Laurence A. Steinhardt," pp. 40, 48.

38. "Dear Mother," 13 Aug. 1944.

39. Moorad, "Baba Walks a Tightrope," p. 6.

40. "Dear Family," 29 Sept. 1944.

41. "Dearest Mother," 15 Oct. 1944.

42. "Dear Dad and Mother," 18 June 1945.

43. "Dear Lillian," 26 Sept. 1944.

44. "Dearest Family," 26 Aug. 1944.

45. "Dear Mother," 14 Oct. 1944.

46. "Dear Lillian," 7 Sept. 1944. Barry Rubin argues, "Ankara was jokingly called a diplomatic concentration camp.... Each summer, government officials and foreign diplomats fled Ankara's baking heat, sandstorms, and sirocco wind on the overnight train for the cool breezes of cosmopolitan Istanbul" (*Istanbul Intrigues*, p. 1).

47. "Dear Family," 6 Sept. 1944; "Dear Kids," 7 Sept. 1944. It is a bit surprising that Havreberg did not include "squat toilets" on her list of inconveniences; rather, she candidly reported, "The Turkish toilet is very simple—two slightly raised foot rests and a drain. Also, there are sometimes clogs for those who don't wear shoes" ("Dear Lillian," 7 Sept. 1944).

48. "Dear Mother," 14 Oct. 1944.

49. "Dearest Family," 26 Dec. 1944.

50. "Dear Lillian," 7 Sept. 1944.

51. "Dear Mother," 14 Oct. 1944.

52. "Dearest Mother," 12 Mar. 1945.

53. "Dear Lillian," 26 Sept. 1944; "Dear Family," 26 Sept. 1944.

54. By contrast, Ellen Clarkson, Havreberg's travel companion and Ankara roommate, did not adjust well to the city and submitted her resignation in late September. "Dear Lillian," 26 Sept. 1944.

55. "Dear Mother," 28 Aug. 1944.

56. "Dearest Family," 26 Aug. 1944. Biographical information about the life and career of Antoni E. Balinski prior to World War II can be found in an untitled and unsigned typescript in the Jenkins Papers.

57. "Dearest Lillian," 21 Feb. 1945.

58. "Dearest Family," 11 Jan. 1945.

59. "Dear Mother," 14 Oct. 1944.

60. "Dearest Dorothy," 4 Jan. 1945.

61. "Dearest Family," 5 Feb. 1945.

62. "Dear Lillian," 21 Aug. 1945.

63. "Dear Dad and Mother," 10 Sept. 1945.

64. "Dearest," 9 Apr. 1946. With the heightening of Cold War tensions, the United States continued to encourage Turkey to remain firm on sole control of the Turkish Straits. In 1947, funds from the Truman Doctrine provided Turkey with $100 million in economic and military aid. An additional $300 million of Truman Doctrine aid was granted to Greece. Between 1948 and 1951, Turkey received an additional $137 million in aid from United States funds provided by the Marshall Plan. David Welch, *Modern European History, 1871–2000: A Documentary Reader* (London: Routledge, 1999), p. 129; Martin Schain, *The Marshall Plan: Fifty Years After* (New York: Palgrave Macmillan, 2001), p. 120.

65. "Dearest Family," 6 Sept. 1944.

66. "Dearest Family," 31 Aug. 1944.

67. "Dear Family," 21 Sept. 1944.

68. "Dearest Mother," 12 Mar. 1945.

69. "Dear Family," 21 Sept. 1944.

70. "Dear Mother," 14 Oct. 1944.

71. "Dearest Pat," 18 Nov. 1944.

72. "Dear Mother," 20 Apr. 1945.

73. "Dear Dad and Mother," 10 May 1945.

74. "Dear Dad and Mother," 14 Aug. 1945.

75. "Dear Lillian," 20 Aug. 1945.

76. "Dear Mother," 24 Oct. 1945.

77 "Dearest Pat and Du," 24 Oct. 1945.

78. "Dear Mother," 16 Dec. 1945.

79. "Dearest Lillian," 3 Jan. 1946.

80. "Dear Lillian," 10 Feb. 1946; "Dear Mother," 22 Feb. 1946; "Dear Mother," 6 Mar. 1946.

81. "Dear Mother," 19 Apr. 1946. *See* the Appendix for a copy of this special order.

82. "Dear Family," 25 May 1946.

83. Ibid. On the deaths of the nine babies aboard the *Holbrook, see* Jenel Virden, *Good-bye, Piccadilly: British War Brides in America* (Urbana: University of Illinois Press, 1996), pp. 73–74.

PART I Washington, D.C., 1936

Washington, D.C.

January 5, 1936

Dear Mother:

I don't see how I am going to find time to write letters at all. I'm so happy about everything.

Have just finished reading the *Redfield Press* for January 2. Had a grand dinner at the house today—turkey, dressing, sweet potatoes, kernel corn, pickled peaches, celery, olives, fresh baking powder biscuits and ice cream with chocolate sauce on it.[1] They have pancakes every Sunday morning but Gladys and I slept late. . . .

Gladys is a grand girl for a room mate for me. She is very sensible. She teaches music at Junior High School—1200 students. She has taught there for three years and goes to night school two nights a week as she is working on a masters.

I pressed my clothes yesterday afternoon and the iron isn't bad at all. Mr. Blount told me to take the day off yesterday and get settled so I did.[2] Had a very good sleep last night. The weather is so warm we had two of the three windows wide open.

My knees bothered me terribly on the train and it seemed I just couldn't suffer in silence because I had to tell Mr. Norbeck about it. They ached so much and sometimes it was almost impossible to sit through a meal. I think it was because I sat in the same position so much. I didn't intend to tell you if they kept on feeling that way but now I can tell you truthfully that I feel perfectly swell and my knees don't hurt at all—even in the morning; and I'm so glad.

I'm in the office all alone now. Mr. Blount is going to give me some work this afternoon, but he left a few minutes ago and I guess I'll get the work when he comes back. . . .

The Senator said that he was taking me to church next Sunday—when he found out I didn't go this morning. On the way down from Norbecks' yesterday morning we stopped in some park to look at the statue of Jeanne D'Arc Aux Femmes d'Amerique, Les Femmes de

France. The Senator didn't ask me any questions about her—simply told me to get a book on Joan of Arc and read it—in about a week he's going to ask me some questions about her.[3] He hasn't forgotten either as he mentioned it again today. I intend to do it all right. Guess I had better get one today. . . .

We make our beds only once a week—Sunday morning. They have a couple of darling colored boys waiting on tables at the place where I stay. . . .

Messy letter isn't it.

Much love,

Marge

Jan. 5 [1936]

11:30 P.M.

Hello sweethearts:

Mr. Blount didn't come back after all but I stayed at the office all afternoon and read newspapers. Josie came back after dinner and at six o'clock we walked over to the station to send a wire and then to the post office.[4] From there we took a street car to the downtown post and walked several miles. We stopped at the Mayflower Hotel and walked around the lobby. It is the most luxurious place I have ever been in.[5]

A lot of the Senators were in there. . . . Josie and I window shopped all along the way and we were about famished at 7:30 so we stopped at the Garden Shoppe and had waffles and sausages.

Came home on the street car after that. Washed out some clothes and talked with Gladys and now I'm tired.

Much love,

Marge

[P.S.] The grass is green here you know and they have stands out doors on the streets with cut flowers. I am told that a dozen roses can be had for 25¢ and in the spring for 15¢.

Didn't get my book on Joan of Arc but will have to do that tomorrow. . . .

125 B St. S.E.
Washington, D.C.
January 6, 1936
Dearest Lillian and Duke,[6]

. . . Went to work this morning at about 8:30. Gladys is as bad about getting up in the morning as I am and the same about going to bed. I feel so darned lucky to have her for a room mate—I like it much better than having a room by myself.

Took an hour off at noon and managed to find my way down to the dining room and back again without getting lost.

Mr. Blount complimented me on my work tonight. I work for him altogether. I turned out quite a stack of mail but they were almost all short, simple letters. The spacer doesn't work right on my typewriter and my shoulders ache from turning the roller by hand but I came home gloriously tired—washed my face, combed my hair and went down to a good dinner—not as good as yours and Mother's but good. . . .

That Joan of Arc stuff makes me mad but it's funny too. I remember the general story but I don't know what he's going to ask me so I'll have to plan to spend tomorrow night at the Congressional Library I guess. I can see it out the window and it's all lit up like the Union Station. It looks like another of those places with endless halls that look alike and are so easy to get lost in.

Get such a kick out of these poor congressmen. They have to look at everyone and I bet if I said "hello" they would shake hands and greet me like a long lost friend. They seem to think everyone is one of their constituents. . . .

It's nine o'clock—must take my bath–
Lots and lots of love,
Marge
[P.S.] Am anxious to hear from all of you.

≁ 125 B. St. S.E.

Washington, D.C.

January 7, 1936

Dear Dad,

Left home a week ago tomorrow. Have you missed me?

The AAA decision by the Supreme Court yesterday seems to be causing some excitement and a lot of uneasiness on the part of its 6000 employees.[7]...

Little Congress met tonight. I intended to go over but Carrie, Gladys (my roommate) and I were talking. I really don't talk much I just listen. Carrie discusses world affairs, politics, and anything with fluency.

Gladys knows all about music. They're both very intelligent and I feel like a ninny around them. They are really grand girls though and I feel lucky to be living here with them.

Little Congress, I forgot to say, is an organization of all the stenographers and secretaries on "the Hill" and that makes me eligible to join. I'll go the next time they have a meeting to see what it's like. Gladys says it is very interesting—they debate on all the questions that come up in the real Congress.

Have to *work* on the newspapers for awhile now and go to bed.

Have a date with Josie for 9:30 next Sunday morning to go to Sunday School. Makes me sleepy just to think of it because I like to sleep on Sunday.

Must go to bed now with my newspapers.

Lots of love,

Marge

[P.S.] The weather is still grand here. I cannot get used to this kind of weather in January. My coat is much too warm.

≁ 125 B. St. S.E.

Washington, D.C.

January 8, 1936

Dear Mother,

... Sally [Selma ("Sally") Norbeck, the senator's daughter] went to lunch with me today and we stopped at the Congressional Library. Was astonished at the elaborately decorated interior. The mosaic work is beautiful. Was glad to have Sally with me the first time and I don't think I'll get lost in there as it is planned in such a way that it's very easy to get around. Got my Joan of Arc books and have been reading one of them tonight.

Three of the girls from upstairs came down after supper. Very nice girls but my Gladys and Carrie are the prizes. I don't believe there are two girls in this house from the same state.

Must go to bed now with my book and newspaper.

Much love,

Marge

125 B St. S.E.

Washington, D. C.

January 9, 1936

Dearest Mother,

Was so darned happy to get your letter today. . . .

It rained off and on all day today. Rainy weather is the typical winter weather here—Sally told me. It is still very warm—not summer weather—but a little warmer than April in S.D. or perhaps the same. You should have heard the whistles and seen the astonished looks when I told [them] that it was 31 below in Redfield at 6 A.M. Are you sure you read the thermometer right? . . .

I have more money than I need. I get my first pay check next Wednesday and I still have $20.53. I have kept track of everything I've spent and I really don't need very much. I will have to send all I can spare home for the next 6 weeks to pay my debts and after that I'm going to put away $50 to get home on and then I'm going to buy a suit. I could have sent part of the $20 home to you but if you don't need it I'll wait until I get paid so I can send a larger amount all at once. . . .

Sally took me over to the room where they are conducting the investigation of Morgan and Lamont concerning credit extended to the allies at the beginning of the World War. I believe it's the Senate Munitions Committee that is doing the investigating for the purpose of a new neutrality act or plan or something. Haven't read my newspapers enough. Anyway we sat about ten feet from J. P. Morgan and Lamont. Morgan has about the biggest face and head of any man I've seen. He seemed to rather enjoy the whole thing—he would laugh a lot and was very much pleased with himself. There were about 40 newspaper people there and pictures were being taken all the time.[8] . . .

Thank you for your good wishes, Mother—and I sincerely wish the same things for you.

Lots of love to all of you,

Marge

[P.S.] I'm going to take a good hot bath now, fix my fingernails and take Joan of Arc to bed with me—Goodnight, dears.

125 B St. S.E.
Washington, D.C.
January 11, 1936
Dearest Lillian,

This is the third letter I've started to you since last night. . . .

Incidentally I took the dictation and transcribed the biggest bunch of letters today that I have ever done—at least it looked like more so I counted them and there were almost sixty. Most of them were short so that doesn't mean very much. Mr. Blount said when he gave me the letters that they were very fine and it was good work. I know you will be glad to hear this.

Yesterday noon Mr. and Mrs. Jenkins stopped at the office. Mr. Blount told me to leave with them and I wouldn't need to come back until two o'clock. We had lunch and a very nice visit. I felt so much more at ease with them than I ever did with Tommy [Havreberg's former fiancé] around. I like them both very much. Mrs. Jenkins apparently doesn't know the present situation but Tommy will probably tell her when he finds out I'm here. . . .

I can feel that there are so many more opportunities to really do something here than I did at home. I may not do any better but it makes life a little exciting and much more interesting . . . .

I think I'm just so lucky to be here with such really nice girls. I don't mean nicey-nice—Carrie brought some port wine in tonight. They all smoke occasionally but they can take it or leave it. Things haven't been easy for them either—they've all been around and know what life is about but they are very good natured and I enjoy listening to them. . . .

How's the bridge? Most of these girls don't play bridge. They play

"Monopoly" when they play cards.[9] We're going to play it soon. It sounds like a real estate business when they explain it—buying, building and selling. . . .

Goodnight dear and lots of love,

Marge

✈ 125 B St. S.E.

Washington, D.C.

January 13, 1936

Dearest Mother,

Waited 15 minutes for the mailman to come this morning [before heading to work]. Thought sure I would get a letter from home but nary a one. Why doesn't someone write to me? I hope everyone's well. You don't need to have some news—just write and say anything.

Had a grand time yesterday. It was a perfectly beautiful day. I got up at 8:30 and went to Sunday School and church with Josie. Enjoyed it very much. Just as I was coming home for dinner Sally came up and I went down to the cafeteria to have a cup of coffee with her and the Senator. Then I came home and had dinner with Gladys, Carrietta, and Frankie—I think they are the nicest girls in the house. Sally came at 3:00 o'clock for me and we spent some time—about 40 minutes— looking at the Greek sculpture work at the Corcoran (or something like that) Art Gallery.[10] Beautiful work and as I haven't had any ancient history at all I will have to spend some more time at the library. Then we went up to Sally's boyfriend's apartment. His name is Clarence so Sally calls him C. K.–his initials. He's tall and quite good looking but he has a mustache. He's very nice though. He went with us and we drove across the Potomac River and into Virginia. Visited Lee's home.[11] It closed just a few minutes before we got there so we couldn't go in but we looked in the windows. It's a beautiful place and I simply fell in love with the huge cedar tree in back of the house. Maybe Lillian remembers it. Then we drove through Arlington [National] Cemetery and stopped at the tomb of the unknown soldier. There is a large amphitheater I believe that is dedicated to all soldiers. It's a beautiful thing and is supposed to be a copy of the old Greek amphitheaters except this has marble benches.

From there we went to the apartment of some friends of Sally's. They have been married only a few months. I liked them both. We left there at about 7:50 and Sally and C. K. brought me home. I hadn't had any supper so I went down to have a sandwich. Gladys had to go over to the library so I went with her—we went into the newspaper room and she read the Pittsburgh paper and I read the Aberdeen [South Dakota] paper, but I couldn't find anything in it except Washington news. . . .

Both Frankie and Gladys think I should meet some young people, get a party dress and have some fun. Frankie was plotting and planning the other night and last night when Gladys started saying the same things I accused her of having talked to Frankie, but she said she hadn't. Gladys wanted to know if Sally's boyfriend wouldn't get a date for me but I really didn't think so—however, Sally must have heard us because today she said C. K. has a friend of his all picked out for me and she says all the women are crazy about him. Then, he has another fellow in mind too so maybe I'll have a date one of these nights. . . .

Gladys is going over to Little Congress with me tomorrow night.

A week from Sunday I'm going to hear the Vienna Choir Boys with Carrietta.

I am also going to Norbeck's church with them a week from Sunday. . . .

Should wash clothes tonight and take a bath, but I washed my hair and my towel isn't dry yet.

How is the well drilling business coming?

Please write once in a while. Tell Lillian to be sure to write too.

Goodnight and all my love,

Marge

125 B St. S.E.

Washington, D.C.

January 19, 1936

Dear Mother,

I've been having the grandest time. I realize I haven't written for several days and I'm terribly sorry.

Friday afternoon the whole office force was invited to the horse show at Fort Myer.[12] Josie didn't go but Mr. Gjolme, Mr. Blount, Sally and I went out.[13] Harrison King, an officer at the Fort and son of Harry King, got the tickets for us. I had never seen anything like it before and enjoyed it very much. The horses were beautiful and Sally and I decided they had more intelligence than their riders. They had some of the most complicated drills and they did them awfully well.

One noon last week Sally had to go down town so we went down and had lunch at a drugstore counter and honestly those boys work so fast and there were so many people in there I was all worn out when we walked out just from watching them. From there we went into one of the department stores and I wanted to get some pajamas so Sally took me down on the electric stairway. I had never seen one before and Sally practically pulled me onto it. She was so surprised that I hadn't seen one before and she said she wouldn't have pulled me on that way if she had known.

Last night Josie, Mr. Blount, and I were invited out to Norbeck's for dinner. Josie didn't go but Mr. Blount and I went out and Sally had asked me to stay overnight and go for a hike with her today. We had a delicious dinner. I thought the meals were swell here at first and they really aren't bad for a boarding house but they do get tiresome— I'm beginning to know what we'll have on certain days. After dinner last night we took the Senator and Mrs. Norbeck to a lecture and we went back to do the dishes—then Mr. Blount took Sally and me to "Professional Soldier" at the Fox [Theater].[14] We had an awfully good time—it was a funny show and got us in sort of a silly mood. Then we took Mr. Blount home and on the way to Norbeck's we stopped at a drug store to have a coke. It was raining awfully hard and we had to run across the street to the drug store. On the way back I slipped on the curb and sprawled out on the sidewalk with my arms over my head. It was so darned funny—of course, if I were naturally clumsy it wouldn't have been so funny. . . . I tore a hole in my stocking and was all splashed up with mud and stuff even my hat. Norbecks stay at the Kennedy-Warren.[15] . . .

Got up at about 10:30 this morning and dressed while Sally took her folks to church. It was snowing—something like tiny white hale or is it hail stones—but Sally and I put on old clothes and no hats and walked all around the Rock Creek Park where they have the [National] Zoo.[16] Saw all the snakes, elephants, bears, seals, monkeys, lions, etc., etc. Spent about three hours there and when we got back we took hot baths. Then Mrs. Norbeck, Sally, and I went out for dinner and had fried oysters but I don't like oysters yet. That was about 4 o'clock. After that we read and Sally had to come up to get the Senator at 5 o'clock so she brought me home. . . .

Must get to work—

Lots of love to all of you,

Marge

125 B St. S.E.

Washington, D.C.

January 22, 1936

Dear Lillian:

There is really not so very much to write about at the moment but you are probably wondering what has happened to my letter-writing.

It has been grand, hearing from all of you so often. . . .

Forgot to tell you last week that Governor Tom Berry was in the office one day for a few minutes. He had on his ten-gallon hat and looked like his pictures.[17]

Monday night Carrietta, a friend of hers, Frankie, Gladys, and I played Monopoly. It's a very popular Washington game. Carrietta had popped pop corn and made pop corn balls the night before so that is what we had for refreshments.

Gladys, Carrietta, and I have tomato juice every night before going to bed—it costs us about 3¢ apiece per night for a whole glass full.

P.M.

I got Mother's letter this noon and it was the best letter. She said they had been up to your place for dinner and you have no idea how hungry that makes me. As I said, the meals are pretty good at my place but they are beginning to taste alike.

7:30 P.M.

Back at the office. This is the first time I have worked at the office outside of from 9:00 A.M. to 6:00 P.M. and I haven't worked very long either. Josie and I are going down to see "Tale of Two Cities" tonight and we'll be leaving in a very few minutes but as it has been such a long time since I last wrote I thought I would send a bit air mail.[18] . . .

Have to go now. This is a lousy letter. Sorry.

Lots of love to all of you,
Marge

✈ 125 B St. S.E.
Washington, D.C.
January 27, 1936
Dear Mother, Dad, Lil and Duke:
I really shouldn't be taking time to do this as I have lots to do but I suppose you have been wondering what has happened to me. . . .

Friday afternoon Sally asked me to go to the Horse Show at the Fort again. Josie declined that is the reason they asked me to go again and I enjoyed it as much as the first time. . . .

Went to church with Norbecks Sunday. Wegners from Pierre are here so they were at church too. I went down on a street car and met Sally at church.[19] It is a very nice church and they have a fine pastor.

Carrietta and I went down to Constitution Hall to hear the Vienna Choir boys yesterday afternoon. They were just darling and I've never heard such singing. . . .

I work from nine until six with an hour off at noon. I haven't been asked to work any outside that but I have come back about three times although I haven't stayed long. . . .

I'm still having the time of my life.
Hope you are all well.
All my love,
Marge
[P.S.] No, Mother, I had only a coke the night I fell down. . . .

✈ 125 B St. S.E.
Washington, D.C.
January 30, 1936
Dearest Lillian and Duke,
You'd never guess where I've been tonight. Went to a concert at the Chamber Music Auditorium in the Library of Congress. . . . Despite the fact that I know nothing about music I really enjoyed [it]. It was a queer looking group of people—but very interesting looking people—very high I.Q.s—I hear so much about I.Q. around these

school teachers—in case you don't know—it stands for intelligence quotient. Gladys says the people who attend those concerts are the intellectuals of Washington. I know intellectual is an adverb but you know what I mean. The composer, Quincy Porter, was present in the audience—he is only 39 years old but he looks about 45 or 50. Has gray hair and is very distinguished looking.[20] Mrs. Norbeck told Sally to give the tickets to Josie and me. Josie wanted to work tonight so Sally told me to ask one of the girls here to go. I knew Gladys would like to go as it is only by invitation that one can attend those concerts. She enjoyed it very much. Sally and her mother were going to dinner someplace so they couldn't use the tickets. . . .

It's midnight already—we've had our tomato juice and Gladys is studying. I wish you could meet Frankie, Gladys, and Carrietta. I think they're just grand. . . . [They] make me want to get ahead. I wanted to at home but I couldn't do as much about it as I can here. I could have, of course, at home too there isn't really a good excuse for not doing it, but it's just the atmosphere or the feeling of hopelessness I have at home that I don't have when I get away. I can't really understand the reason for that but it is really the situation. Another thing I know and that is that I don't intend to remain single all my life. You don't know how lucky you are to have a husband—and still luckier that Duke is your husband. . . .

Mr. and Mrs. Jones [owners of the Betty Alden Inn], Carrietta, Gladys and I are the only ones living on this floor. Eight girls live on the floor above us and four girls, a married couple, and a boy live in the other side of the house—it's called "the other house" but it's really adjoining.

I don't know why I write so much about nothing.

Much love to all of you,

Marge

125 B. St. S.E.
Washington, D.C.
February 3, 1936
Dearest Lillian:

I don't know why I've been carrying my letters to you around without mailing them. Things are beginning to pile up on me—things to write about, I mean—and as a result, I don't get anything written. . . .

I don't know about working for the Senator anymore after this session. If you will remember when he suggested my coming here he definitely stated it would be for one year only so I won't ask him to let me stay longer but that doesn't mean I can't get another job here. Can't take time to go into it now but you needn't worry, I'm thinking about it. There is more to it than that though—one year may be all I will want here but I do hope I will make use of the opportunities that are here. It might be nice to go to the West Coast next year or some place in the South—I haven't quite decided yet, there are so many places a stenographer could go. Stenographers are quite in demand here. The girls told me that when some of their offices opened here they needed them so badly that finally they didn't pay any attention to their politics but hired Republicans as well as Democrats.

This was the night I intended to register at night school but had to come back to the office for a few minutes and it broke up the evening for me. I will tell you more about the possibilities of going to night school later. I really have to pull myself away from here now and go home.

Lots of love to all of you,

Marge

125 B. St. S.E.
Washington, D.C.
February 8, 1936
Dear Mother:

The cookies and candy arrived today and they are simply delicious. I ate four cookies this noon and two pieces of candy—and an orange. The paper was almost torn off the package but the boxes weren't broken. Those cookies are certainly fancy looking and they taste as good as they look. And I didn't know you could make such good candy. . . .

My intentions to write at least every other day have gone the same as keeping track of everything I've spent and keeping daily notes. There is really no good excuse for not taking at least a few minutes every day to write home and I'm terribly sorry. I will try to do better. . . .

I worked Thursday night for a while. Wednesday evening I was tired and slept all evening; then I couldn't sleep half the night. Thursday evening—we'll skip that. Guess I might as well tell you on second thought. I went to a lecture on Christian Science by Peter [V.] Ross from California. We got there twenty minutes early but the main part of the church and the balconies were full so there was nothing to do but sit in the Sunday school room in the basement—that was packed too before the lecture began. The speaker was brought down and introduced but we had to listen to the whole thing by an amplifier (can't be bothered to look up the spelling). It was not nearly so impressive as being able to see the speaker would have been—it was really more like listening to it over the radio—except I concentrated more than I would [on] any radio lecture. I really didn't miss a word of it but couldn't hope to get more than a few of the principles the first time. I really think it is wonderful though. I don't think you or Dad would care about it and I think another religion would be better for Lillian but it is the thing I need.

Had a lot of fun last night. Frankie, Gladys, Carrietta and I went over to Fourteenth Street to the bowling alley—The Arcade. They have all played a lot, of course, but I hadn't and I thought it was so darned much fun. At first I thought it would be just a game of chance for me—I mean just luck if the ball even stayed in the right alley but it was just lots of fun. Afterwards we stopped at a cocktail room and had a Sidecar. Never had one before and they're certainly powerful.[21] Please do not get the idea that Carrietta, Gladys, and Frankie go in for that sort of thing in even a small way because they don't. One occasionally is very nice they think but Frankie and Gladys, being school teachers, never know when they might run into one of their kids.

Monday was icey (I guess it is icy)—thick smooth ice. I wasn't two steps out of the house before I sat down. Haven't fallen down since then but have gone through some awfully cute capers some times. Mr. Gjolme fell down that same morning with more disastrous results. He had to have five stitches taken in the back of his head. He had them taken out today and has missed only one day at the office. He stayed at the office almost all day the day he fell down although Mr. Blount tried to send him home. I thought people had to go to bed after having anything like that—but I'm living and learning I guess.

Night before last we had fifteen inches of snow and was that a treat. I haven't seen that much snow even in South Dakota for ages. People were walking who wouldn't think of walking on a nice day because they thought it so much fun. It took the streetcars hours to get any distance at all. They closed the schools at noon—only a few of the students were there in the morning. Everyone was late to work if they got there at all. Big trucks drove down the sidewalks and all kinds of negroes [*sic*] and relief workers were shoveling the snow onto the trucks. It started thawing this noon and this place will be a mess when it really thaws.

It's six thirty and I really must get home or they won't give me any dinner. I would like to send this air mail but the planes aren't going out as another storm is coming.

Love to all of you,
Marge

125 B St. S.E.
Washington, D.C.
February 20, 1936
Dear Folks:

. . . Tuesday night Sally and I went out to Constitution Hall to hear Nino Martini sing.[22] Everything I had read about him was so disgustingly conceited that I thought I wouldn't like it at all but I wanted to go because it is a part of Washington that I want some of. However, I thoroughly enjoyed it. His voice is wonderful and much to my amazement—amazement is too much of a word for what I mean. Rather I noticed that neither radio nor vitaphone really do justice to a good voice and even though I don't know anything about music I can really enjoy good music well played and sung.[23]

Wednesday night Carrietta had some tickets for the Agricultural Department's orchestra's concert. It was just like a large city's band concert but it was pretty good. They had to change the arrangement of their numbers because the piano player didn't come until the thing was half over or more and everyone laughed when she finally came in. . . .

Oh yes, Friday night I went up to Norbeck's for supper. I didn't ask Sally what I should wear, but I have worn this red knitted dress on every other occasion that I had gone up there and I just couldn't wear it again anyway. I was sure it would have been terribly inappropriate so Friday noon I went down town and bought a dress. A dress that is entirely different from any I have ever had. I was so afraid I would be sorry afterwards because I got it in a hurry and it cost $14.95. It's a pussy willow taffeta—print. Size 14 and fits perfectly. I can't describe it but gray shoes and hat will look grand with it. It's rather dark print black and gray and sort of violet and cerise or something. I can't explain it. The sleeves are full and gathered at the top—they just cover the elbows. It has a collar that comes down to points, buttons—tiny buttons covered with the material of the dress—down the back and a very clever tie in front. It has a wide black suede belt with a large buckle covered with the same material as the dress and the dress has pleats in front. I was never so glad that I had bought anything in my whole life after I got up there and I felt very much at ease all evening. . . .

Say, Mom, do you have a coat yet? They have wonderful bargains here and now is the time to buy winter coats. I think I could get a nice one for you here. Please let me know right away quick.

All my love to you dears,

Marge

[P.S.] I've decided to work in South Dakota if I can just to be near the family and keep track. I don't think you tell me everything about the difficulties—in fact you don't tell me anything about them. . . .

125 B St. S.E.
Washington, D.C.
February 22, 1936
Dearest Lillian:

I owe so many letters now I don't know how I will ever catch up. . . .

I don't believe I told you that Sally and I went over and watched Mrs. Huey Long sworn in—that was almost two weeks ago, I believe.[24] Too bad I don't keep you advised from day to day as I imagine it would be interesting to get it fresh. Mrs. L. looked very nice. She has an awfully nice smile and everyone seems to like her very well. She was appropriately dressed in black—she has a nice form. She wore an orchid on one shoulder and when she and her colleague walked down to the Chair somebody whistled "Here Comes the Bride." The galleries were packed and after she was sworn in practically everyone left. I think the "Here Comes the Bride" came from the Press Gallery. They walked down so nicely that the tune was a very nice accompaniment although it could just barely be heard—Sally couldn't hear it at all.

Went to a National Geographic lecture last night at Constitution

Hall.[25] Josie and I went. It was on New Zealand and that may not sound a bit interesting but really we enjoyed it so much. There was really very little lecture as it was practically like a travel talk—motion pictures and vitaphone. I'll tell you all about New Zealand when I come home.

Much love to all of you,

Marge

125 B St. S.E.
Washington, D.C.
February 22, 1936
Dear Folks:

... I think I had better give the long looked for report on New York before I go into anything else. I certainly wish I had a typewriter.

Sally, her friend (C. K.), Edith Norbeck, Sterling, Helen and I left here at 12:20 last Saturday night. I had intended to take a nap that evening but had to go back to the office. We took two double seats across from each other and had a lot of fun all the way up. They use the oldest coaches they have on the excursion trains. We didn't sleep at all all the way up and we got awfully hungry and I had a couple ham sandwiches with no butter on them—some of the kids got some of the coffee—it had sugar and milk in it and tasted like rat poison. We weren't supposed to get in until about 5:50 Sally thought, but we arrived at Pennsylvania Station, New York, at 4:30. It was a huge place but all of a sudden we all felt suffocated—I suppose it was the damp stale air. C. K. carried a brief case with tooth brushes, extra stockings, etc. We brushed our teeth and had tomato juice before going out into the street. It was still night of course and all the stars were out. We walked from the station down to Times Square—practically no signs were lighted and the streets were practically deserted except for some taxi cabs and we saw a few couples in evening clothes—high hats and everything. From Times Square we went down to the subway. We took an express from there to the Battery—if you know what and where the Battery is and I don't expect you do.[26] ... You pay your nickel of course as you go through the gates on your way to the station. Everybody going out and in goes through the same doors at the same time—that makes just a swell mess and a whole lot of pushing. The doors are opened only a few seconds and I suppose if anyone gets caught in the door they are simply caught. No I guess they could get in or out but I wouldn't try it.

When we got out to the Battery we paid another nickel to go out to Staten Island on the ferry—the ferry was a big thing but the water was so smooth I did not experience any special feeling of being in deep water. We went past the Statue of Liberty and out to the Island. Everybody runs to and from subways and ferries and things so when we stopped at the Island we all ran up and out and turned around, put our nickels in and ran all the way back. Fun! On the way out we all tried to see the New York sky line as it was quite light out but everything was sort of gray and foggy. New York was out of sight before we reached the Island, of course. We saw Ellis Island too . . . but it wasn't anything to see. . . . On the way back Helen and I stood up in front watching for New York and things. We looked around and C. K., Sally, Sterling, and Edith were all sound asleep. . . . Then Helen and I went over and joined them. We fell asleep too—it was impossible to stay awake with the gentle shaking of the boat and being tired in the first place. That was the longest day. I can't hope to cover all of it but will try to tell you the high points. Eventually, at about eight o'clock, we went to the Automat at Times Square for breakfast.[27] I expected an automat to be a cheap tinny place but this one, which is the nicest in New York, was really very nice. The food was not expensive but very good.

Along about now we went out to Brooklyn to the dock where the Norwegian boat, the *Stavangerfiord*, was docked. . . . It isn't large but it goes across the ocean and I think I got a bigger thrill out of it than anything.[28] It was the *only* ocean-going ship in New York last weekend. . . . It was just like a visit to Norway for me—because there wasn't anything American about it. We tried all the doors and walked into every stateroom we could—we saw all three classes. There were a bunch of men who work on the ship down on the third class deck—it isn't really a deck—as that part is below water level—I think. Anyway there isn't a promenade deck around it. Not one of us could talk Norwegian and I was never so sorry. Sally wouldn't attempt it. One of the cooks talked a little broken English and he took me into the room where a machine peals potatoes. I asked him if he made "pootakaka" but he pronounced it "pootatushaka."[29] Only one of them could talk English very well and he had charge of the refrigerator down below. He asked me if I could talk Norwegian and when I said no he said, "You should be ashamed."[30] He was awfully nice [and] asked if we would like to go to Norway to ski and then brought out a bunch of pictures of himself and others skiing in Norway. He showed us the room just packed with Norwegian cheeses and then the other foods that were stored down there. He also took us to the room where they have the engines and everything. It was a huge place. I can't imagine what one of those big ships looks like. . . .

Just like I wanted to spend all day on the boat, I wanted to spend all night writing about it. . . .

All my love,
Marge

125 B St. S.E.
Washington, D.C.
February 26, 1936
Dear sweet Mother:

. . . Monday night Gladys, Josie and I went out to [Theodore] Roosevelt High School to hear a lecture by Carl Sandburg. I remember studying some of his poems in High School. I remembered "Chicago" especially and when I was in Chicago I kept thinking of that poem and how well it expressed Chicago all the time I was there. He was very interesting and had a perfectly beautiful speaking voice. He talked for a while on Lincoln's period compared to the present (he has written a very good book on Lincoln), read some of his poems, and sang some folk songs.[31]

Last night I had a blind date. A friend of Franky's just returned to Washington and she was at the house for dinner the other night so I met her. Her boy friend had a friend and she wanted to know if I would care to double date some time just for fun. She said he was very nice and knowing Franky so well and as Franky was sure Charlotte (the girl) was very nice I said I would go. Anyway Charlotte called Monday night and wanted to know if I would care to go out Tuesday night so I said I would. She told me he was very young—he is about half a year younger than I. Wait until I describe him. His name is Robert Byron Harbeck and he has the reddest coppery colored hair I have ever seen and it's curly. His face makes me think of Stan Laurel of "Laurel and Hardy."[32] He is tall—believe it or not, dresses very nicely and has a nice car—I drove it home at about 12:30 on account of I wanted to drive in Washington and there was hardly any traffic at that hour. We went to a night club called the Lotus. Now this is funny. We went in and sat down and the waiter wouldn't bring us our cocktails until Robert Byron Harbeck (strangely enough called Red by everyone) could prove he was twenty-one. He managed to prove it by showing his driver's license but the poor boy was so embarrassed. Charlotte and her friend are about 25. We really had fun dancing and talking. They are nice kids. Red asked me for a date for Saturday night and I told him I would go if I didn't have to work so he will call me Saturday afternoon. Since then I remembered that that is the night Mrs. Jones is having a party for all the girls at the house so I think that as long as she is nice enough to do that we should be nice enough to attend so I don't think I will have a date that night. Franky said she would prefer to have the cobwebs swept off the walls and new wallpaper put up than have Mrs. Jones give a party to cover up the shortcomings. Mrs. Jones is really very nice though and she isn't an ordinary rooming house keeper. They used to have a good deal of money. I think she is awfully sweet and Franky has been sort of nervous lately, school teaching is hard on the nerves and now she has enrolled at G. W. (George Washington University) so she is busy working on her Masters.

To get back to the business of dating. There are about ten girls to every boy in this town and the town is full of old maids. It costs a lot to take a girl out here and, I understand, most fellows who do take them out expect a lot in return. So Red, having a car and being so nice, is really worth knowing. Anyway, I would just as soon go with him once in a while, if he asks me. . . .

In case I haven't told you I get $150 a month. Isn't that wonderful. I will be completely out of debt when I get my check Saturday. Sally thinks I have done awfully well but when I think of all the money I have had in the past two months it seems as though I've spent an awful lot. I've started cutting out the concerts, although we always sit in the gallery seats [where] it costs about a dollar and a half. It seems like I spend a couple dollars every time I go outside of the house and

I don't go out any more than the others. I do eat lunch every noon and it seems awfully extravagant but it's a hard habit to break and it's always twenty or twenty-five cents—for a roll, a vegetable, and a glass of milk or a cup of coffee. Going to New York cost about $12.00 and although it was worth it I can't see how I spent that much—the ticket was $3.50, seemed like we rode subways all day—Sally and I decided we must have spent about $2.00 in nickels on subways. Edith and I really got soaked on our supper. We went over to the New Yorker after taking the tour of Radio City to meet the rest and we were awfully hungry.[33] The cheapest thing on the menu was scrambled eggs and bacon for 60¢, then the waiter asked us if we wanted toast and coffee, we rather assumed the toast wouldn't be extra and the coffee couldn't be much. They brought a silver coffee pot for each of us for 20¢ and some toast for 20¢ so a couple pieces of bacon, a bit of scrambled eggs, and toast and coffee cost us $1.00 apiece and then we had to tip. Boy I was exasperated....

The last two days have been simply wonderful—so nice and warm. It smells like Spring and looks like it. They say the Cherry blossoms will be out in about three weeks and the magnolia trees on the Capitol grounds will be in blossom. I think it's the magnolia trees they said.

I am so glad that it's warming up in South Dakota. We have been watching the weather in the South Dakota papers and it must have been terrible. Everybody freezing their legs and everything. It makes me feel guilty for not staying home and sharing it a little....

I have been thinking a lot about how nice it would be to go home but I'm afraid if I go home I'll be stuck again and Franky and the kids I was with last night really believe I could get a job here. I know several things to do about it. If I can, of course I will stay and if I do that I hope you folks will come down this summer....

Oh there is so much to write about but I've simply got to quit.
All my love,
Marge

→ 125 B St. S.E.
Washington, D.C.
March 5, 1936
Dear Mother and Dad,

. . . Wednesday was a beautiful day—just like summer and Wednesday evening was simply perfect. Now I know I'll have to tell you about John. He's the night elevator boy and I like him better every day but I don't know where it will get me. Now you can understand that I don't mind working evenings. I have found out quite a little about him in snatches of conversations with him. He is from Massachusetts and he's a medical student. In one more year he will be a doctor. He's about 25 and is attractive—nice looking—his hair is dark but not black. His eyes, I think, are a very dark blue. He would love to go out west where you can see the country as he loves to walk. He goes to church every Sunday and I must find out what church he goes to. He has to go out on obstetric cases for a month this summer but he gets a month's vacation. Medical students have to work at it every minute of the day so he doesn't get any time off for relaxation. I think he must be engaged because he's too nice not to be. It's all kind of silly but fun to be interested in someone. . . .

Tonight Josie and I went down to the 14th St. shopping district and I got some shoes finally. I got black patent leather strip pumps—size 7 ½ quad so they fit—$5.50. I will have to get a suit or a coat or something when I get my next check. I haven't bought any clothes but the dress, hat and shoes, and I do need something so badly.

All my love,
Marge

→ Washington, D.C.
3-11-36
Dearest Mother:
Received your letter tonight.

Sent Lillian a birthday card today and it won't get there until Saturday. Thank gosh Saturday is pay day.

Didn't go bicycling Sunday after all—Sally went alone and I slept. Did get up and go to church though. After church we had a regular session of meeting people and talking to them. Sally, Mrs. Norbeck were there. . . .

Jil and I went to Little Congress last night and walked around for a while after that. . . .

I have been writing all the time that I have so much to tell you but just haven't time. Thought I'd write a few words tonight—on the eve of my twenty-second birthday. . . .

The South Dakota society is having their dinner Sunday. I guess Sally and I are going after church. I hate like the devil to pay $1.25 for dinner there though and miss dinner at home. I think I'll talk to Sally about that. . . .

All my love to you,
Marge

✈ 125 B St. S.E.
Washington, D.C.
March 16, 1936
Dearests:

I just finished a three weeks' wash and nearly rubbed the skin off my knuckles. It is nine o'clock and I'm going to spend the next two hours writing to you.

When I was taking dictation Thursday morning the mail came in and there were so many things for Josie we wondered if it could be her birthday. Believe it or not, it was and she was as surprised as I was to find our birthdays were the same day [12 March]. I didn't tell the kids ahead of time because I was afraid they would make a fuss about it. I asked Josie to come over and have supper with me that night because we should celebrate together but she suggested going down to the Madrillon for supper where they serve a $1.50 supper for $1.00 on Thursday nights.[34] They had a floor show, too, of course. I had shrimp and crabflake cocktail, consommé, omelet with shad, roe, and mushrooms, spinach, chifonette salad, and French pastry with rum in it. We ate from seven o'clock until nine. We walked around for a bit and then Josie came up to the office and I went home. When I went home to change my clothes at six o'clock, I told Gladys that it was Josie's and my birthday. When I got home at about ten o'clock Carrietta, Gladys, and Frankie were in our room and there were two packages for me on the dresser. One was a little doll on top of a bunch of mints tied up with cellophane. In the other package was one of the new Yardley compacts with rouge, lipstick and loose powder. It's a lovely thing but I didn't want them to do anything for me. They made me feel selfish for not telling them because they said it would have been so much fun for them too to plan something special and we could have had a table downstairs fixed up for dinner that night with a birthday cake and everything. I am kind of sorry now that I didn't tell them because it would have been fun for all of us and I did want to eat dinner with them that night but Josie didn't care to.

Friday night I packed my dress and stuff in the small case from my suit case and Sally picked me up. Mrs. Norbeck had a tea that after-noon so we had little sandwiches and cakes for supper. I ate about a dozen sandwiches I think. We cleaned up there and picked up C. K. and my date whose name was Glenn Sompfin (or something like that). He is tall, dark, has a moustache, and wears a derby. Sally liked him because he reminded her so much of a fellow at college that she had so much fun with. I liked him all right and he seemed to fit in with the rest of the party very well but he wasn't interesting. That is, he regis-tered practically nil with me. . . .

I slept late Sunday morning—until 9:30; had breakfast and cleaned up for the S. Dak. Society's dinner at the LaFayette [in the Hay-Adams Hotel]. I think I told you I didn't want to go but Sally thought I should go but she said I didn't have to, of course. Anyway I went and had a grand time. Sally had to arrange for cars to go out to the Wash-ington [National] Cathedral after the dinner so she was terribly busy. There were about two hundred or more there and she knew practically everyone and if she didn't she did before the afternoon was over. Every State in the Union has a flag at the Washington Cathedral and S. Dak. didn't have one before last Sunday so everyone went out to see the presentation of the flag. . . . I met so many people I can't remember half of them. . . . Bill Bulow's (South Dakota senator William J. Bulow's son) wife asked me if I was related to the Havrebergs who used to live at Beresford. She knew them before Aunt Minnie died. . . . Mr. and Mrs. Bulow, Mrs. Norbeck, First Assistant Postmaster [William W.] Howes of Huron and his wife, Mrs. Werner, and I think [former South

Dakota congressman] Royal Johnson and his wife and I can't remember who else were in the receiving line. . . .

It's eleven o'clock and I'm afraid I won't have another chance to write this week as I'm going to be busy every night until Sunday and that always takes care of itself. Haven't time to tell you all I'm going to do.

All my love, Marge

125 B St. S.E
Washington, D.C.
March 22, 1936
Dearest Lillian,
It's twelve o'clock and a h— of a time to start a letter. . . .

Went to the National Geographic lecture Friday night as I have been to most of them. . . . It was on birds—especially birds that are nearly extinct. The name of it was something like "The Microphone Takes After Lost Birds." It was a motion picture with sound effects and a Professor from Cornell talked. It was very interesting. They had our meadowlark in it too and it made me think of Spring at home.

When Gladys and I came home we talked until late—reminiscing. It made me think of someone and I went to sleep thinking about him and woke up thinking about him. By noon I recovered. Really, that must be one of the main reasons I like it here and I'm so happy is because I'm meeting new people all the time and haven't time to look back. The Senator will never know what a godsend his offer was.

Went downtown yesterday noon looking for a suit. Sally was looking at dresses too and when we were about ready to leave Jellefs [women's clothing store], she espied a dress on the rack and let out a whoop—took the dress and me into the fitting room and in about ten minutes I had bought the dress. It's an evening dress and I'm crazy about it. . . . Sally says she will have a party special so that I'll be sure to have a chance to wear it. And, of course, there will be the S. Dak. Society's spring dance to wear it to. . . .

Sally and I were both so excited about it and when we were in the fitting room I told her about Mr. Blount's thinking I could get in at the Veteran's Bureau so I might be here all summer and then Sally told me the Senator wanted me to work again next year if everything goes as he expects it will. Today the Senator told me that too but he couldn't promise for certain. . . . And to think that I couldn't even get a job that paid 60 or 80 a month before. . . .

Lillian, how is everything at home? I'm afraid you tell me only the good things. I can do something about it now in the way of money. . . .

It's so late I must go to bed. Good night, dear.
Love,
Marge

✈ 125 B St. S.E.
Washington, D.C.
March 24, 1936
Dear Mother,
And tomorrow's your birthday and I didn't send you a card. . . .

The Senator left today. He will probably ask you if I've written often when he sees you.

Please send letters to me care of the office (362 Senate Office Bldg.) after this as Norbecks have asked me to move up there and live with them until they close the apartment which will be about May 15th. After that Sally and I will get a room someplace until she leaves which will be June 15. I will pay the same room and board that I do here and of course it will be grand to live at the Kennedy Warren. I hate to leave here though and I wish I could live both places at once. Sally is going to teach me to drive in Washington too so in case I'm here next year that will be part of my work. . . .

The cake and cookies came to the office yesterday. I gave everyone a piece there and they all thought it was swell. Mr. Blount came back and said, "Your mother certainly knows how to make cake, tell her to send that kind all the time—it beats angel food or any other kind—Do you have any more?" So I gave him another piece and Josie wants the recipe—I can't remember it. Will you send it? . . .

Must go to bed but there are some other things I wanted to write about but can't think of them now.
Lots of love,
Marge

>[{] 362 S. O. B.
Washington, D.C.
March 28, 1936
Dearest Lillian:

Gee it's a beautiful day. The trees are beginning to blossom and it's grand out. A man on our street has a big basket of flowers—one of these nights I'm going to stop and buy a bunch. . . .

These educated people seem to think you should go to school just for the pleasure of it and it is a lot of pleasure all right. I think I would really like to. . . . I have been thinking I would love to take Art and English. I would really enjoy both those subjects and I need the English badly. . . .

Carrietta says they need stenographers at the Resettlement [Administration] and Josie said there were four ads in the paper the other night for stenographers. . . . I have been thinking too that I might be able to get a job at Bill's bank in Bismarck for the summer and come back here in the fall. . . . Unless something goes wrong I'm pretty certain of having this job again next year. . . .

When you think my letters sound blue you may be sure it's because I'm tired and not because I'm blue. I never feel that way anymore. . . .

I heard there was a dust storm in South Dakota last week. I hope they don't start again. It rains so often here and everytime it does it makes me just sick that it can't be that way in South Dakota.

Loads of love,
Marge

>[{] Washington, D.C.
March 30, 1936
Dearest Mother:

In about five minutes the Doctor is going to take me home. Now I'll keep you in suspense for a couple days waiting to find out how I like him.

When I asked him to mail the letter to you for me, he asked me how long I would be working and I told him until about ten-thirty. Then he asked if he could give me a ride home. He told me his car was in Massachusetts (his home) sometime ago and I know he hasn't been up after it so this must be someone else's.

I was so excited when I came back in here I called up Gladys to tell her and she said, "It must have been the hat," because I wore my half a hat tonight.

It's a grand night but he always talks about "beautiful operations" and he likes to fix cars and things too. He's just a fine fixer, I guess. Maybe he can fix a broken heart too.

Love,

Marge

P.S. I don't sound much like a broken-hearted girl though, do I? I'm glad, of course.

1024 Kennedy Warren
Washington, D. C.
April 3, 1936
Dearest Lillian,
. . . Have so much to write about this week. It's late and I'm simply exhausted. I took a hot bath and it seemed to ooze out the last bit of strength I had and left every muscle relaxed and I'm in the grandest bed I've ever slept in in my life. It is Mrs. Norbeck's. She has taken the Senator's room and Sally and I have this room with the twin beds in it.

I wrote to Mother Monday night and told her John was going to take me home. That was sort of leaving you in the air for a few days. I left the office at 10:30 and he was waiting for me. He had someone else's car—I think it was a Ford roadster. He started driving to the house and then asked me if I wouldn't like to go for a ride first—it was a grand evening. We rode down through Rock Creek Park and just rode all the time. He wanted to know if I would like something to eat but I didn't want anything so we just kept riding—the only time we stopped was when we stopped for a split second to light a cigarette. At 12 o'clock we were down near the Tidal Basin and he said he would like to have me see his school at Georgetown and wanted to know if it was too late, but I said I would love to go over so we drove over there. I enjoyed the evening immensely. We just talked and laughed all the time—sometimes we were serious but most of the time we were silly and it was fun. He was simply swell. It was one o'clock when I got home. He teasingly asked for my telephone number so he could call me in the morning and get me out of bed. I didn't think he would but he did. I had been up about ten minutes when he called and I told him I'd been up for hours. Carrietta and Gladys nearly had fits when they heard me talking to him over the telephone at the crack of dawn after being with him the night before....

Yesterday afternoon I received a letter with the request to burn it. I took it in the john and lit a match to it then dropped it in the toilet. The darned seat was wood covered with enamel and it flamed up. I worked frantically putting out the fire. I didn't call anyone until I got it out and I was just shaking—I singed my hair a little and I was kind of sooty. I called Josie in and she was so darned sweet about it. She said her mother did the same thing once. She didn't think they would even make a charge for it. They clean the office every night so she thought they would just report it to the superintendent of the building, and he would have it replaced without any comments or questions. I didn't make any explanations for burning the letter or say who it was from. I knew Sally would discover it so I told her. I was embarrassed and blushed terribly—even my ears were red but it was funny. Sally thought it was the funniest thing and we laughed and she teased me. I didn't think Mr. Blount would go in there as he had been using the one in the Senator's office but he came back in a few minutes and of course he went in there. Sally and I held our breath and when he came out he was laughing and said, "Who tried to set the world on fire." I had to leave then as I had to go downtown before the stores closed to get my dress. After I left Sally said Mr. B. said, "Poor kid." I told him I would pay for it, of course, but it was replaced this morning and Josie said they thought the maids did it but they didn't think anything of it. I don't suppose I'll ever see one of the things without thinking about it.

The fire started Sally and me off for the evening. We were going to the Shoreham with C. K. and Jim so we had dashed madly downtown at noon to arrange for shortening my evening dress.[35] It cost $2 but I didn't have to bring a slip as I wore my half slip.... We took our time dressing and when I finished honestly it seemed as though I looked like someone else. Jim is the same one I had a date with for Sally's waffle supper. His name is Jim Reed and he's a lawyer at the Dept. of Justice. He's about 30—not good looking but he looked very nice last night—in tails—in case you don't know, white tie means tails and black tie, tux—most of them have both. Tails, of course, is strictly formal. He had a high hat too that was a lot of fun to play with—you know smash it down and then pop it up. It had his initials in it too so it wasn't rented.

My dress was a lucky strike. I don't think I'll ever buy anything again without getting Sally's advice on it. I told her I would send cables to Sweden next year for advice on clothes.[36] C. K. said, "Say Marge, did you win the Irish sweepstakes," and I asked why and he said I looked like a million dollars. Jim was very sweet to me and I think it must have been the dress because he wasn't that way at the waffle supper but at that time I was still awfully shy. I'm still quiet a lot but have acquired a little confidence or maybe it's just a false front I don't know. Anyway Jim says that dress really does me justice and he likes my hair this way.

April 4, 1936

Had to quit and go to sleep last night so will continue from there. Will have to make it brief now though. I like Jim now. We had so darned much fun that night. First we went to the Wardman[37] and danced, then we went over to the Shoreham to dance. I told you Jim didn't register before because he and a couple other fellows spent most of the evening discussing some of the government's investigations and stuff. He is a lawyer at the Department of Justice—attended Harvard but didn't acquire the Harvard accent or whatever you call it. His having attended Harvard scared me out for a few minutes but we were having so much fun and he was so nice that I soon got over it. Sally and I were as silly as a couple nuts all evening. We felt just grand and honestly it was so much fun. At about two o'clock we went to Jim's apartment at the Kennedy-Warren and he fixed scrambled eggs. He and another fellow that I like awfully well have an apartment together. Mario (pronounced Mar'-e-o) Monetti is the name of the other one. He's Italian. Mario is from California and works in McAdoo's office.[38] . . .

Jim called this afternoon and asked me to go to the races with him—they're in Maryland or Virginia or someplace—anyway I was working so he asked if he could come up after me at six-thirty and we would do something. I couldn't turn him down again because he was so much fun that I would like to go with him once in a while and Gladys won't mind—I'll go over to see her tomorrow, so I said he could come up. Jim took us to work Thursday morning too. Mario called in the morning and said, "This is Mr. Reed's secretary, etc., etc." It's a lot of fun. What? Just everything.

April 5, 1936
. . . We went to church this morning and then drove around the Tidal Basin with a few thousand other people to see the cherry blossoms. . . .
Lots and lots of love,
Marge

Washington, D.C.
April 6, 1936
Dearest Lillian,
. . . Mr. Blount told Sally today he was going to do his best "by hook or crook" to get a job for me when Congress adjourns. . . .
Washington is getting lovelier every day. I wish I could send you a blossom from a magnolia tree. Have you seen them? They're so big. It seems as though every kind of tree in Washington blossoms and it's lovely.

They are beginning to turn the fountains on—the ones at the Reflecting Pool were turned on yesterday. On Sundays the parks are full—the Zoo is like a circus—children with their fathers and mothers or nurses and there are people out riding horseback or bicycling or just walking or riding. It's so much fun.

I have driven the car for Sally a couple times. I parked for the first time today and I did it perfectly. I wanted to take a picture of it I was so proud. . . .

There are so many things to write about. I'm leading such a happy, carefree, selfish life I feel guilty. I haven't done anything to deserve it—I'm just lucky I guess—
Lots of love to you dear,
Marge

Washington, D.C.
April 14, 1936
Dear Mother,

I came back tonight to clean up my work but I am just aching to write to you so I'll take time out to do so. I thought I would hear from you today but I didn't. I haven't written for a week and had a couple letters from you last week so I guess I shouldn't be looking for one. . . .

They're holding a Civil Service stenographic & typing examination next month and of course I'm taking it. . . .

Last Tuesday night Sally and I came back to work. I left—went downstairs to mail some letters and talked to John for a while. He said he called me one night at the Betty Alden but I had moved. Sally and I wanted to do something goofy—I suggested wading in the Reflecting Pool but that was a little too goofy so she took the car out and called C. K. He suggested going bowling so the three of us bowled. Played two games and I made better scores than the last time. I called John on the telephone and he recognized my voice over the telephone which surprised me very much. I guess he doesn't have any girl friends who call him up or he would never have taken a chance like that—I mean saying my name without knowing for sure who it was. It was such a grand night I asked him if he would like to ride around for awhile after work. He said he would love to so we picked him up at eleven. Sally liked him better than she thought she would—he always seemed so terribly serious minded to her but he's a lot of fun. We rode over to Mount Vernon but it was too dark to see much. I thought it a coincidence that the next day I received a letter from Lillian asking me why I didn't have John take me over to Mount Vernon sometime. John left for Massachusetts—his home—the next day for Easter vacation and he hasn't returned yet.

Wednesday noon Sally took me to the Senate Daughters luncheon. They meet every week and Sally has asked me before but I always begged off. . . . I had met all but one of the girls that were there before and they are all nice. I had to laugh to myself—at how it would sound in South Dakota—when one of the girls said, "I'm getting so I just hate Paris." They were talking about Sally's going to Europe this summer. This girl went on to say that when they took their trip around the world last year they spent one-fifth of their expenses for the entire trip in 24 hours in Paris. There were only five girls at the luncheon that day. . . .

We went to church, of course, Sunday morning. Oh yes, I forgot to tell that Easter around here is almost like Christmas. They make a lot of it. Mrs. Norbeck has a whole stack of Easter cards and Sally bought a bunch of flowers for her and I bought an Easter Lily plant with Sally for her mother. Mrs. Norbeck has insisted that Sally shouldn't get anything for her and then we found stockings under our pillows with Easter cards from Mrs. N. . . .

Mrs. Norbeck had the office force up to dinner last night. I drove them home and I was afraid they would all suffer from indigestion after my driving them home. But Sally told me to drive and afterwards she told me I did a beautiful job of it. . . . Mr. Gjolme left soon after dinner and Mrs. Norbeck, Mr. Blount, Josie and I played bridge. I enjoyed it a lot and they seemed to too because they didn't leave until 11:30 and after that Mrs. N. and I did the dishes.

Jil called me the day I was sick and I hadn't called back so I called her this morning and we had lunch together at the Supreme Court Building and took her around it afterwards. The fellow that took me around runs an elevator over there and he recognized me so he kept getting people to take us into different rooms that ordinary tourists don't get into. He sent us into the library without anyone and an officer was about to put us out and I told him I was from Senator Norbeck's office—after that he let us stay and took us around a little. That's the first time I have pulled anything like that but I found that it works charms. Sally got a kick out of it and told me to use it any time. . . .

The way I blow off in these letters—I'm getting too cocky. I need my ears knocked down a little. Going from the depths of last fall to the heights this year—it's kind of hard to keep my balance.

Best love to all of you,

Marge

P.S. I thought I missed something. I forgot to tell you about yesterday—Easter Monday. Everybody goes Easter egg rolling. The colored people go to the Zoo to roll their eggs and the white people go to the White House. Everybody fixes up a basket with Easter eggs dyed and candy eggs to eat and lunch and they go for all day. There were egg rollers all over the Capitol grounds and all over the Washington Monument grounds and the White House grounds were packed. Grown-ups aren't allowed without a child under fourteen. Mrs. McIlway fixed up a basket for John and he came down to the S.O.B. [Senate Office Building] for Sally and me. The officer at the gate of the White House was getting sort of cross as everyone was pushing and he couldn't let more than a child and a grown up in at a time. The child was supposed to be with his mother. When we got to the gate John told him Sally was his sister and he said I was with him too—he tried to say I was his sister too but as I went past the officer said, "I suppose she is just fourteen too." So I got in as a youngster. Mrs. Roosevelt appeared but not while we were there. We played catch with our eggs and when we had broken a few we ate them. Had a lot of fun watching the mob. It was a very gay and colorful crowd. Everyone was dressed up in their best and they carried balloons and they had a boys' band playing and a magician doing tricks and everyone had a swell time. The day was grand for it. I don't know whether they roll eggs on Easter Monday anyplace else but it has been an annual event here for years and years. It's sort of silly but they all seem to enjoy it a lot.[39]

Must go my bus leaves in about five minutes.

Goodnight, dear,

Marge

+ Washington, D.C.

April 22, 1936

Dearest Mother:

Surprise!!!! I'm coming home and I'm as surprised as you are. I may not get to Redfield for a month but I'm leaving here a week from tomorrow or possibly on Friday, May 1. Received a letter from Harold [Norbeck] reading, in part, as follows:

As Sally has reported what a grand time you and she are having in Washington the last few weeks, you won't be happy to have this letter. Dad wonders if you can come out here [Mayo Clinic, Rochester, Minnesota] to handle correspondence? If you can come out, you can ride back with Mother and myself.[40] . . .

I have been having so much fun I really hate to leave but it will be grand to see all of you . . . . I don't know what has happened to me—I do too—I've developed a sense of humor or a light heartedness or something and I hope I don't lose them in South Dakota again. Sally has brought it all about—I'm really her product. She's such a peach—I just hate to leave her. We had next month all planned and I was looking forward to going up to New York to see her off but now I'm going to meet her when she comes back next year. I simply think she's swell in case I haven't told you a dozen time before and tears come to my eyes when I just think about leaving and all the fun we have had. . . .

I haven't finished my sight seeing. I think I'll get Jim to go up the Washington Monument with me. He suggested it last week—or rather that I take him sight seeing. He has been here a year or maybe several but lots of people have lived here all their lives and haven't done any sight seeing. Funny, isn't it?

I must get to work now, have some stuff I want to finish up and I'm taking dictation all day tomorrow—rather I'll be working on it all day.

Must get to work.

Lots of love and I'll see you soon,

Marge

✈ Damon Hotel

Rochester, Minnesota

July 2, 1936

Dear Lillian:

. . . I expect to take the Civil Service examination here next Monday but don't expect to be needing a job for some time—although I don't know how long. . . .

We've been having grand weather and Rochester is a very pretty town. It has lots and lots of hotels and every other hotel is a hospital. The hotels are a lot like hospitals too—nurses coming and going all the time.

Mr. Blount came this morning. It was nice to see him again. He has asked me to have dinner with him at the Kahler tonight. The Kahler is the swankiest hotel in town and Harold says dinner costs $1.50 or $2.00 there. I'm afraid I'll get indigestion. That isn't much for the East but it seems like a lot out here.[41]

I'm getting frightfully restless. Wish I could go back to Washington now. I'm really content—I mean I like the work and the Senator is a peach—but I'd like to go to dances, learn to swim, play tennis, bicycle, ride horseback and lots of things.

It's time for the Senator's supper.

Take care of yourself, dearest, and

Lots and lots of love,

Marge

Marjorie Havreberg was at Senator Norbeck's bedside in Redfield, South Dakota, when he died of throat cancer on 20 December 1936.[42] She would work for a time in Pierre, the state capital, marry Paul Steinbach in 1938, and temporarily put aside her desire for dances and other things. Even though the couple moved to Washington, D.C., to work, it was not a happy period in Havreberg's life.

NOTES

1. Havreberg lived at the Betty Alden Inn, a small boarding house for young working women located at 125 B Street Southeast, during most of her stay in Washington.

2. Julian Blount was the private secretary of Senator Norbeck. *See* Gilbert Courtland Fite, *Peter Norbeck: Prairie Statesman* (Pierre: South Dakota State Historical Society Press, 2005), p. 97.

3. The statue of Joan of Arc, by Paul DuBois, can be found in Meridian Hill Park.

4. Josie was a co-worker at the Norbeck office.

5. The historic Mayflower Hotel, which opened in 1925, is located on Connecticut Avenue in downtown Washington, D.C. Its lounge, with elaborate gold trim, has long been a gathering place for Washington's social and political elite.

6. Floyd ("Duke") Enstrom was Lillian's husband. He owned and managed a family shoe store, Duke's Bootery, in Redfield. Leta Ann Nolan, *History of the Spink County Area, 1889–1989* (Dallas, Tex.: Curtis Media, 1989), p. 114.

7. In an effort to reduce the crop surplus and raise crop prices, the Agricultural Adjustment Act, enacted on 12 May 1933, restricted agricultural production by paying farmers to reduce crop acreage. The money for these subsidies was generated by a tax on companies who processed farm products. On 6 January 1936, the Supreme Court ruled that the AAA was unconstitutional for levying this tax. Congress enacted the Soil Conservation and Domestic Allotment Act in 1936 to replace the AAA. Herbert S. Schell, *History of South Dakota*, 4th ed., rev. John E. Miller (Pierre: South Dakota State Historical Society Press, 2004), p. 289.

8. Between 1934 and 1936, the Senate Munitions Committee, led by Republican Senator Gerald K. Nye of North Dakota, investigated reports that armament manufacturers had unduly influenced the American decision to enter World War I. This investigation helped spark the adoption of neutrality legislation in the mid 1930s. J.P. Morgan, Jr., and Thomas W. Lamont, Jr., a close associate of Morgan who became chairman of the board of J. P. Morgan & Co. in 1943, were two of the more than two hundred witnesses called to testify before the committee.

9. Charles Darrow invented the game Monopoly in 1934 and sold it to Parker Brothers in 1935. The game's promise of fame and fortune made it especially popular during the Great Depression. According to Hasbro, its present owner, more than one billion people have played Monopoly.

10. Today, the Corcoran Gallery of Art in Washington, D.C., founded in 1869, is a major center for historic and contemporary American art, although its collection also contains ancient pieces.

11. The home of Confederate General Robert E. Lee, called Arlington House, is now a national memorial.

12. Fort Myer, which traces its origins to the Civil War, is a United States Army base adjacent to Arlington National Cemetery in Virginia.

13. Hans Gjolme was a childhood friend of Peter Norbeck who worked for the senator. Fite, *Peter Norbeck*, p. 13.

14. *The Professional Soldier* was a 1936 adventure movie starring Victor McLaglen and Freddie Bartholomew.

15. The Kennedy Warren apartment complex was the Washington home of many wealthy congressmen and senators. For more on the Norbeck family and their household, *see* "Lydia Norbeck's 'Recollections of the Years,'" ed. Nancy Tystad Koupal, *South Dakota Historical Collections* 41 (1978): 21–128.

16. Rock Creek Park, founded in 1890, is an urban park that extends twelve miles from the Potomac River to the border of Maryland. It was one of the first federal parks to be established in the United States. The original National Zoo, founded in 1889, is located within Rock Creek Park.

17. Democrat Thomas ("Tom") Matthew Berry was governor of South Dakota from 1933 to 1937. Schell, *History of South Dakota*, p. 381.

18. *A Tale of Two Cities* was a 1935 movie based on Charles Dickens's novel of the same name.

19. The Norbecks' oldest daughter, Nellie, had married Lester Wegner of Pierre, the capital of South Dakota, in the summer of 1927.

20. Quincy Porter (1897–1966) was a prolific American composer, who would win the Pulitzer Prize in 1954.

21. The sidecar is a cocktail made with cognac, orange liqueur, and lemon juice. The first recipes appeared in 1922.

22. Constitution Hall, a lecture and concert hall built by the Daughters of the American Revolution, opened in 1929. Nino Martini (1905–1976), a tenor, began his career in Italy and moved to the United States, where he starred both in movies and at the Metropolitan Opera in New York.

23. Vitaphone was a sound process in which sixteen-inch phonograph records contained the soundtrack for movies and were attached to the projector.

24. Rose McConnell Long was the widow of well-known Louisiana politician and United States Senator Huey Long who had been assassinated on 8 September 1935. Rose Long was appointed to fill her husband's seat on 31 January 1936, becoming the first woman from Louisiana to serve in that position. She won a special election on 21 April 1936 to serve out her husband's term, but she would chose not to run for reelection in November 1936.

25. The National Geographic Society regularly presented films and lectures at Constitution Hall during the 1930s and 1940s.

26. The Battery is located on the southern tip of Manhattan facing New York Harbor. It got its name from the artillery batteries positioned there in the seventeenth century to protect the settlement of New York.

28. Automats, or restaurants in which coin-operated vending machines dispense simple food and drinks, were popular in the 1930s and 1940s. The growth of the suburbs and drive-through fast-food restaurants in the 1950s and 1960s led to their decline.

28. The SS *Stravangerfiord,* built in 1918, carried many immigrants from Norway, Sweden, Denmark, England, and Ireland to the United States and Canada. After forty-five years at sea, it was sold as scrap in 1964.

29. This version of potato latkes is made with grated potato, chopped onions, and olive oil, which is mixed together and fried.

30. Both Havreberg and the Norbecks were of Norwegian immigrant stock. In South Dakota, many first and second generation immigrants grew up speaking Norwegian, learning English when they went to school.

31. "Chicago" appeared in Carl Sandburg's first published collection of poems, *Chicago Poems* (1916). Sandburg's enormously popular *Abraham Lincoln: The Prairie Years* was published in 1926, followed by *Abraham Lincoln: The War Years* in 1939.

32. The comedy team of Stan Laurel and Oliver Hardy began making movies during the late 1920s and 1930s.

33. Radio City opened in Rockefeller Plaza on Sixth Avenue in 1932, while the New Yorker, on Eighth Avenue, opened in 1930. At the time, the New Yorker was the largest hotel in the city with as many as five restaurants.

34. The Madrillon was a well-known supper club where famous jazz, swing, and Latin musicians performed during the 1930s, 1940s, and 1950s.

35. Since 1930, the Shoreham Hotel in Washington, D.C., has played host to presidents, world leaders, and inaugural balls.

36. Sally Norbeck would leave soon for Stockholm to continue her training as a medical technician. "Lydia Norbeck's 'Recollections,'" p. 123.

37. The Wardman Park Hotel (now the site of the Marriott Wardman Park Hotel) had opened in 1916 to help meet the demand of the influx of government workers during and after World War I.

38. William G. McAdoo served as the Democratic senator from California from 1933 to 1938. During World War I, he was secretary of the treasury under President Woodrow Wilson.

39. The Easter Egg Roll on the White House lawn on Easter Monday is a tradition dating back to 1878. In 2010, an estimated thirty thousand tickets were distributed, with participants assigned to one of five different time slots.

40. Senator Norbeck had left for Mayo Clinic in Rochester for treatment of throat cancer in March. He would convalesce in South Dakota. Havreberg would remain

with the ailing senator for the next eight months, both at the Mayo Clinic when he went for treatment and in South Dakota. During the last months of Norbeck's life, she acted as both his nurse and secretary. "Lydia Norbeck's 'Recollections,'" pp. 123–26.

41. The Kahler Grand Hotel, located directly across the street from the Mayo Clinic, opened in 1921. During the 1930s and 1940s, the Kahler Hospital occupied the top floors of the hotel.

42. Fite, *Peter Norbeck*, p. 205.

Senator Peter Norbeck stands on the steps of the Senate Office Building in Washington, D.C. *South Dakota State Historical Society*

The Norbecks stayed at the Art Deco-style Kennedy Warren
apartment complex when they were in Washington, D.C.
*Louise Taft Oswood photograph, Historic American Buildings
Survey, Library of Congress*

President Franklin D. Roosevelt attended the dedication of Mount Rushmore on 30 August 1936. Among those in the front row of the seating area are Mrs. Lydia Norbeck, center with hand to face, Marjorie Havreberg in black hat next to Mrs. Norbeck, and Peter Norbeck, third from right with a bandage around his neck. *South Dakota State Historical Society*

Marjorie Havreberg (left) stands with Paul Steinbach
and Sally Norbeck, possibly in Washington, D.C.
Jenkins Collection, South Dakota State Historical Society

Havreberg wrote regularly to her parents, Henry and Bessie Havreberg, in Redfield, South Dakota. *South Dakota State Historical Society*

(*top*) Ankara in the 1940s resembled a typical city in
the West, with wide, tree-lined streets and modern buildings.
South Dakota State Historical Society

(*bottom*) The central square in Ankara features a statue of
Mustafa Kemal Atatürk. *South Dakota State Historical Society*

(top) When Havreberg arrived in Ankara in 1944, the city was
a study in contrasts. The old city was built on a hillside and some
women still wore veils. *South Dakota State Historical Society*

(bottom) Havreberg wrote enthusiastically of her encounters
with Turkish peasants, such as these children in the old city.
South Dakota State Historical Society

Havreberg met Antoni ("Balo") Balinski, counselor at the Polish embassy in Ankara, in August 1944. *South Dakota State Historical Society*

Picnics were a popular activity during Havreberg's tour of duty in
Turkey. Here she poses with a generous selection of food and drink.
South Dakota State Historical Society

Patricia Havreberg married George ("Du") DuChateau in the fall of 1945. The marriage was the subject of several letters from Marge Havreberg to her family. *South Dakota State Historical Society*

Havreberg frequently wrote to her sister, Lillian Havreberg Enstrom, shown here during a 1949 tour of Europe. *South Dakota State Historical Society*

Parties and formal affairs were a regular part of foreign service life in Turkey. Attending what may be the New Year's Eve 1945 party are, from left, Corelli Jernigan, Bob Moore, Marjorie Havreberg (then Steinbach), Admiral W. L. Jackson, Bill Ross, and Charlie Tryon. *South Dakota State Historical Society*

Men wore either a top hat, white tie, and tails or full dress uniforms to formal events. Dressed for such an activity are Earl L. Packer, second from left; Colonel Theodore ("Ted") Babbitt, fourth from left; Ambassador Laurence Steinhardt, fifth from left; and Colonel Frederick A. Pillet, sixth from left. Captain Ewart Seager is fifth from the right, partially hidden. Next to him from left to right are Commander George C. Miles, G. Huntington Damon, and Captain William F. Ross in profile. *South Dakota State Historical Society*

(*top*) Corelli Jernigan shared many of Havreberg's adventures in Turkey and remained a close friend after their tour of duty. *South Dakota State Historical Society*

(*bottom*) Virginia Sipp, at work in the military attaché's office, joined the staff a few months after Havreberg arrived. *South Dakota State Historical Society*

(*top*) Havreberg made many visits to the Ankara airport, either to see people off on their trips or to travel herself. *South Dakota State Historical Society*

(*bottom*) Artist Saip Tuna created this crayon sketch of Marjorie Havreberg during her last few weeks in Turkey. *South Dakota State Historical Society*

The men in Havreberg's life posed for this photograph during her visit
to Redfield, South Dakota, in June 1946. From left, Henry Havreberg,
Antoni ("Balo") Balinski, Floyd ("Duke") Enstrom, and George ("Du")
DuChateau. *South Dakota State Historical Society*

This sketch of Marjorie Havreberg was made not long after she left Turkey.
South Dakota State Historical Society

(*opposite*) A young Sally Enstrom plays with Antoni ("Balo") Balinski
and Marjorie Havreberg in Redfield, South Dakota, in June 1946.
South Dakota State Historical Society

PART II Ankara, Turkey, 1944–1946

Marge Havreberg's letters and her adventures resume after her separation from Paul Steinbach. In 1944, she began considering overseas jobs with the State and War departments.

↘ Washington, D.C.
April [30], 1944
8:30 P.M.
Dearest Mother—

I've been dizzy ever since I read my mail tonight. Can't even talk straight and [my roommate] Janett just laughs at me. I took a cup out of the cupboard and then put it down and picked up the saucer and started pouring coffee in it! No I don't have the job and don't be surprised if I don't get it. I knew that they were thorough in their investigations and have been told from reliable sources that an applicant is shadowed from the time they were interested. Often think of it and when I catch a man looking at me, I wonder if he is an investigator. But I have been scared ever since I found that someone actually visited the home town for no other reason. It's just that it makes me nervous to have someone go over my Past with a fine tooth comb and it makes me feel unduly important. They certainly go to great lengths for a piddling job. The base pay on this will be less than I am getting now. . . .

I had the grandest letter from Harold [Norbeck] written April 11th and a State Dept. man had called him at the office that morning. (I am still mystified at how they traced Harold to find his office because I gave only his home address). Tonight I had a letter from Julian Blount—nice one too—that a representative of the State Dept. had called him from the railroad station—he had just an hour in Huron; had been in Redfield and was going through to Rapid City. . . .

Golly I hope I make the grade now—especially when I know how tough it is to get in. . . . Must write some more notes tonight so goodnight dears.

Very best love to all,
Marge

✈ Washington, D.C.
May 14, 1944
Dearest Mother—

Happy Mother's Day and I'm so sorry that this isn't arriving on Mother's Day instead of being written on the day. You will understand and I hope excuse as you read on. I tried to call you today but there was a three hour wait on getting the Minneapolis line so I cancelled it.

I'm getting ready to go to Turkey. Don't fall over in a faint now. I'm thrilled to pieces about it. This is starting at the end—now I'll go back two weeks and lead up to it. It was two weeks ago last night that I wrote to you and it seems like two months at least. . . .

Tuesday morning I had a telephone call from Military Intelligence [a division of the United States Army] asking me if I was still interested in foreign service and if so would I care to go to Turkey. I told them that State had already requested my release to go with them but if the salary was higher with them I would be interested. It is—the base pay is $200 higher so I said I would call them later in the day. Instead I went out there [to the Pentagon] and had a talk—found out the little they knew about it. . . . With the War Dept. I will work in the Embassy and be with the State Department crowd because I will work for the Military Attaché and he is in a sense on the staff of the Ambassador. There is a Military Attaché, and Assistant and four other officers in his office with two American clerks and about five Turkish clerks. The Attaché cabled M. I. D.[Military Intelligence Division] and asked for stenographers, said he didn't care whether they were sixteen or sixty or what they looked like if they could take dictation and transcribe. There is a tremendous amount of work. I liked the sound of that anyway.[1] . . .

For a while I sort of had cold feet on the whole deal and looked around at beautiful Washington—the trees and everything and thought of the comforts of living and the advantages that there are here—and I confess I was frightened for a few minutes. But I also knew that I had very sincerely wanted to go overseas for too long to pass it up and that if I didn't I'm sure it would give me a complex for life that I was a coward and didn't care for anything except easy living and I wouldn't have been worth a d—. I have had no doubts since like that and I know that I will not again and I don't feel that I'm showing a spark of courage either—I'm simply following the line of least resistance and selfishly doing what I want to do too. . . .

I have three weeks training and a few weeks after that I leave. Because you out there don't know how these things work I'll tell you as much as I know and the things everyone knows. There's nothing secret about my going to Turkey—it is a neutral country and my going there has nothing to do with troops. The secret will be when I leave and the route I travel, because that is war time traveling. I will go by air though that is certain. I don't know how long I will be here—it may be a month and it may be two months. From what I have been told it will be more than a month—probably five or six weeks. From the time I am told to leave Washington I won't be able to contact anyone by letter or any other way. I'll go to whatever city I take off from and stay there for a few days, maybe a week, and at each point along the way I may stay several days waiting for transportation on from there. I don't know yet whether they will notify you of my arrival but I'll find out and let you know. Anyway, don't worry about not hearing because the trip may run into three or four weeks and I know you would be notified at once if anything happened—if a plane along the way was long overdue I would be listed as a passenger. That's not likely to happen though and I'm only mentioning it in case you get wild worrying notions because you don't hear—actually if you don't hear you can be certain I'm all right. I am terrifically excited over the trip—even if I shouldn't like the two years in Turkey—the trip alone would be worth it. . . . I might go down to Miami or wherever they go to take off for South America and from there over to Dakar, then Cairo, and up to Ankara. Your guess is as good as mine on the route and I suppose you will have me out of Washington a dozen times before I ever leave just because you don't hear.

If you want to read something about Turkey get Willkie's *One World* and read the part on "Turkey, a New Nation."[2]

Had a long visit with another daughter of Mrs. Mack's today—on the phone—I called to talk to Mrs. Mack and ask more questions.[3] Mrs. Mack was at her "summer home in Maryland" but called me when she came back late this afternoon. I had long visits with both of them. The daughter said if she didn't have a husband and child, that she would be over there too—that Mable likes it so much they think she may never come back, that she is having the time of her life. . . . All the girls are very popular. The daughter told me that it's quite a change from Washington—where there are about fifty girls to every man—over there it is just reversed. Pat, take note. Later when Mrs. Mack called . . . she spent a lot of time telling me all the things to take and things her daughter didn't take that she has asked for later. . . . It's no small task to buy a two-year supply of everything. It makes me dizzy when I think of getting this apartment out of the way and getting clothes and stuff besides—either one alone would be plenty— I'm getting the apartment out of the way first and sending you the rugs, linens, and Mixmaster. Everything else I'll send to [Washington friends] Dee's and Dorothy's for their use or just for storing till I want them. . . .

I've written all this stuff so that you would know what I have gone through and in reading it you may feel when you have finished as certain as I am that it's perfect. And then on the other hand you may feel that I need my head examined. But it is fun. . . .

Loads of love,
Marge

✈ Washington, D.C.
May [15], 1944
Monday night
Dearest Dad,

. . . I'm sending a couple of *Geographic*s I found among our old ones with articles on Turkey.[4] These are written about parts of Turkey where I will not be but may see it. The pictures are good though and it is Turkey. I'm not sending them to alarm you & Mom or frighten you—as far as danger is concerned, don't we face it every day when we cross a street & in a million other ways. When one's time comes it comes! They have earthquakes in California too but no one would stay away because of them. As for invasion—that article was written four years ago & Turkey is still neutral. I'm sending them purely for information—believing you all to be as ignorant about the place as I am. Pat can find more at the library if you want some but be sure to read *One World*.

I'm also sending three of the best maps—on one you can guess with me what route I'll take—another is good for a close up of Europe & the Near East—& the other, the World Map—is really excellent I think—& it doesn't look so far from Redfield to Ankara, do you think?

I am so glad I'm going to Turkey & not to England. Turkey used to be something I had once a year for Thanksgiving—and it's much more than that. I'll have it every day for two years and I'm looking forward to it. I hope you are as excited about it as I am—I'll write often—though they may be only notes & you may not hear for some time from me & then receive several letters. That is the way the mail goes. . . .

My last day as an accountant today & I wasted no time getting that ugly green ink out of my pen. Tomorrow morning I report at the Pentagon Bldg.

I have so much to do. I'm afraid Pat will have to transcribe this for you—I have scribbled so.

Dearest love to you always,

Marge

Washington, D.C.

Saturday A.M.

May [18], 1944

Dear Mom—

. . . The time certainly flies—I'm the busiest thing you ever saw and am I ever grateful to friends—Dorothy especially.

There are so many things to write about & I have so little time.

One box went freight collect insured for $100 on Monday—contains rugs, towels, & odds and ends. The other box went express collect insured for $100 on Tuesday—contains sheets, Mixmaster & odds and ends. I know if I had taken more time or if you could have been here I would have sent other things too and omitted some that I did. Everything else is at Dee's & she's saving them for me. She insisted on paying the transportation of $20 & that helped a lot. Some of the sheets & towels need laundering as you will find. . . .

Have had wonderful luck on my shopping & everything is going along fine—especially the money—I'm keeping track because it will be interesting to have—I haven't been able to buy a raft of clothes—

the main part of the money seems to go for everything else. I got a trunk & duffle bags. Suitcases weigh from 9 to 13 lbs. empty & I don't want to waste that weight on containers.

The office had a surprise party at the apartment one night before it was completely dismantled. Janett knew about it so the apartment was all fixed up with flowers & all. They brought everything—fancily decorated "Bon Voyage, Marjorie" cake & punch & they gave me an overnight bag. . . .

Heaps of love to all of you,

Marge

✈ Washington, D.C.

May [26], 1944

Friday night

Dearest Mother—

You're really a sweetheart. It does take a terrific amount of money but I'm going to make out all right without borrowing any more. . . . I'm so glad I didn't buy a suitcase—I got a duffle bag instead—a suitcase weighs about 10 lbs. empty & the bag (like a big canvas laundry bag) weighs only 1 1/2 or 2 lbs. That weight is precious—because my trunk may take a year to get there although I don't think it will be more than 6 [months]. . . .

I'm going to carry 2 coats over my arm because that won't be counted against my 77 lbs. I'm allowed by plane & get the biggest handbag I can find & carry all the heaviest things in that because that won't be counted either. My clothes I'll roll up in tight rolls & put a rubber band around each for packing in the duffle bag. The girl I'm going with is carrying suitcases & thinks my duffle bag is funny but I think it's smart. I know of a girl who just returned from a trip to the Far East & was allowed only 55 lbs. for several months—she carried a duffle bag.

Mrs. McLarren wants me to take something—a little bottle of perfume—to her girl in Turkey & wants to see me before I go & again offered to help. I'm going up Monday night to see her. Wonder if she will look in her crystal globe for me.

I've been injected for everything—Tetanus, typhoid, typhus, small pox, yellow fever and cholera. Some are single shots, some 2, some

3—I'm through with all except tetanus & I get another shot for that next week—I'm sending you one of my passport pictures. Everyone says it's awful & I hope I don't look as hard as that. Had just been talking & laughing with the photographer & thought I'd better sober up for a passport picture & I guess I did. They are notably bad though & I wouldn't want mine to be different. I wish I had the time & money to have a good one taken before I leave but I don't expect to.

You asked about the girl I'm going with—Ellen Clarkson. She's very nice & we get along fine. Her home is in Blackwood, New Jersey, just outside of Philadelphia. She is *very very* pretty—23 years old but looks a little older than that. She wears a West Point diamond & wedding ring—her husband is dead—probably killed in this war. . . . At least one thing we have in common is we are both of full Norwegian background. Her parents were born in Bergen, Norway. Their name is Hopel—or something like that. . . .

Don't know whether I've answered any questions here & there. Forgive me for not writing more often. I come home at night very tired & then hash things out with Dorothy on what else I need.[5] My list has decreased to only a few things now though. It was awfully hard at first to bust loose & start spending money like that but after the plunge it wasn't so bad. The first few nights Dorothy kept saying I have something you may be able to use, & then diving into a trunk or a drawer & coming out with perfectly lovely things. I don't suppose I should take them but they are all things she either hasn't worn for years, or can't wear because they're too small & they're too nice to give to someone who would not be able to use them for their intended purpose. She has really been a gold mine for me. I may not need them or even be able to use them, but if I do—& from all I've heard I will—it will be wonderful to have changes.

I must get to bed—I thought the money I borrowed would seem a terrific amount to all of you and, Mother, I don't see how you could imagine or guess that it wasn't too much. It's amazing how the little things count up but I certainly won't need to buy anything. Anyway I thought it was awfully swell of you.

Best love,
Marge

✈ Washington, D.C.
June [18], 1944
Sunday night
Dear Mother—

. . . It was good to hear your voices today. When I put in the call the operator told me the lines were down from Mpls [Minneapolis] to Abdn [Aberdeen] so it took some time. I know you think I'm on my way since I called today but I've been so busy & haven't had time to get down town so I wanted to call on Father's day. . . .

Ellen and I get so discouraged. One day it seems that we'll be around for a couple of months & the next it seems we'll get our notice soon. At the moment it's the latter but it's hard to know. We are both so anxious to be on our way & hope that when we do go—we will have to lay over along the way at places & I know that from the moment we leave you are going to worry—& we will probably be enjoying ourselves. It's unfair. Anyway when you do hear that we're gone—don't look for notice of our arrival for at least three weeks. It could be less but please, please, don't worry. It's wonderful to have someone who cares that much about you but worrying is so senseless & there will be no more danger for me than there is every day just in struggling with traffic & what not. I am thinking—very selfishly—of the wonderful & interesting trip & I've seen so many go out & return that there isn't any fear. If I were a man instead & going out to the fighting there would be some difference—but even then, God moves in mysterious ways. When I think of going, the trip & being away for two years I'm excited, happy & thrilled about it but I know it's completely selfish—because I'm not sure that you feel that way. I think you do actually but I also think that you're going to get grey hair—or should I say *greyer*—both of you—waiting for word of my arrival—& I'll be having a perfectly swell time. So when I do write you that I've left—think of me as having a wonderful time. . . .

Must go to bed—washed & ironed today trying to keep my things in shape to go & I pack a little every now & then. I'm about finished on shopping now. Thank goodness & I don't see that I'll need to buy anything for five years & I certainly won't be ready to face the shopping mobs in less time than that.

All my love,
Marge

✈ Miami Beach, Florida
June [25], 1944
Sunday night
Dear Lillian—

Propped in bed—this writing will no doubt be even worse than usual & I know you didn't think that was possible.

Ellen & I have nearly died of boredom today. It's our own fault, no doubt. Did go swimming in the pool. We haven't been down to the ocean since that first day. There are no breakers though so it's not much fun & there are a lot of stingers. The salt water pool here is better & of course there are mats to lie on, umbrellas & deck chairs. But the water is warm—the ocean too—tropical.

There's music all day—good too although canned—but that & the palm trees & the general atmosphere is soothing for a time, but then you get restless. . . .

I'm beginning to think we'll be decorating a palm tree for Christmas before we know it. I won't be able to write when we leave here but it's all the more reason you shouldn't expect to hear that I've arrived at my destination for sometime—because it may be like this all along the way. . . .

It has been a very boring day—after a few of these—it certainly takes the edge off the high adventure.

Best love,
Marge

✈ Brazil
July 4th 1944
Dear Family—

The trip has been perfectly marvelous—I've enjoyed every second of it. Have seen the Amazon River, jungles and more jungles, have slept under mosquito netting, and have seen sunsets and sunrises from above the clouds. I love flying—it's like being in another world. I carried lemons in case I got air sick but I haven't been the least bit so far and I gave the lemons to others who were.[6] Everyone has been so nice—It's much fun and not a chance to get lonesome. No matter how long the trip takes it will be over too soon. . . .

I hope that you are all well. It's been so long since I've heard from you. I wish I had telephoned again before I left to get last minute news of you.

Take care of yourselves & bless you all—

All my love,

Marge

Ankara, Turkey

19 July 1944

Dearest Family—

Just a month today since I left Washington. Arrived at Ankara last Saturday and it was wonderful to find two letters from you. . . .

I hardly know where to begin. I wrote a note to you from Brazil and nothing since till now. I enjoyed the trip although I got sort of tired of living out of a duffle bag. Feel like a veteran on air travel—& I liked it—in fact loved it although at the end of the trip I agreed with Ellen that when I get back to the states I'll use air travel only when I want to get there in a hurry. I didn't get the least bit air sick at any time— Ellen did—in fact said that she has never been sick in her life—but has felt badly half the time since we left the states. Ever since we got here has had what is called gyppy [upset] tummy—which they say most everyone gets soon after they arrive. I haven't had it yet but I'll knock on wood.

I'm going to skip a portion of the trip—and save it for sometime in 1946—& just tell you about Cairo and here. We did have a good time—and everyone was very nice to us all along the way. One thing we found, at least I did—& became more & more convinced all along— that the United States is God's country—and I'm so glad I was born out on the prairies of S. Dak.—in fact my patriotism reached a feverish height long before I got here and has held it. . . .

Only twice since I left have I hit a low and the day we arrived in Cairo was one but I was tired and dirty. After three showers, washing my hair and a full day's sleep though everything looked good again.

I loved Cairo—the name of the place has always intrigued me any-way—like Capetown and Shanghai—and it was just as good as I had hoped it would be. At least part of the credit should go to the guide I had—a person I would have liked wherever I had met him. The first afternoon we went through the bazaars—our pilot, copilot, Ellen &

I. We bought perfume—the basic oil that you mix with 20 parts alcohol to use—Ellen got Secret of the Desert & I got Channel No. 5—& we got one bottle of Taboo to split. You don't do anything in a hurry there—we had to all sit down and drink tall glasses of lime squash while they brought forth every bottle of perfume in the place to smell & then a drop was put on our hands or hair of each until we strongly protested because the place was becoming unbearable. Then after much good natured haggling we settled the price and finally left. . . .

From there we went down the filthy dirty narrow streets jammed full of people—through the bazaars. Saw windows full of gold jewelry, others full of silver, saw silks embroidered with gold or silver and wonderful things. I was too nearly broke to buy anything but I'm going back my first leave—with money and I'll bargain to my heart's content. Ellen didn't much like it and was anxious to get out. . . . Probably I was just in the right mood because I loved it—but I did feel like a bath afterwards. Instead of that we took a cab out to the pyramids. There we had to have a licensed dragoman.[7] It was terrifically hot. . . . I have regretted so many times that I didn't bring a camera with me. I could have gotten films along the way too—& I bought cigarettes—American— at 5¢ a pack all along—until here. A camera is one thing I would like very much to have but [I will] wait till I get some money in my account. It's 20 to 11 and I'll never get through Cairo at this rate. . . . As a matter of fact I think I'd better quit now. There are two very important letters I must write tonight—so they will go out tomorrow. Our mail goes on certain days only—& I want to get these off.

I'm well & happy & please write often. I've never felt better in my life except I think I gained weight on the trip & I don't see how I can keep from getting fat as a tub here—the food deserves a ten-page letter. It's wonderful.

All my love,
Marge

Ankara, Turkey
19 July 1944
Dearest Family—

. . . There is so much to write about but I have to do it in my own rambling incoherent way—& of course it has to be done chronologically. I'll stay at the office & use the typewriter some evenings. Would have tonight but Ellen was sick & stayed home all day so I thought I'd better come home too. . . .

You should hear me speak French—but pity the poor Frenchman who hears me slaughter the language. The Turkish maid in the [Park Palas] hotel who speaks French—the other morning said to Ellen that her French was bad and mine was good. It isn't & the maid's isn't very good either but I felt proud as a peacock—and this morning after I made arrangements—in French—to move to a larger room at the same price—I was about to burst. At least I can make them understand what I want & it's really fun. Last night, Ellen was out & I thought I'd have a lemonade so I telephoned downstairs—the telephone has never been such a hazard before in my life—you never know whether the other end is going to answer in Turkish, French, or the English "hello"—but that "hello" is the extent of the English. The operator must know me because she asked if I wanted Christina—the maid who understands my French—always the way it goes. Then Christina gets on the phone & because we can't see each other's gesticulations it's hopeless, so she says "Entendre! Entendre"—hangs up & in two minutes she's at the door. Last night she came in—I gave her an American cigarette— which incidentally is the most persuasive thing the world over. The little American cigarette can do wonders. Every where you go it's the best backshish (tip or present)—& a pack can do more than a $10 bill. Tell you more of that later. . . .

It's 12:30 & I have to work now. I had nearly 2 months away from routine work. . . .

Goodnight dears & bless you,

Marge

✈ Ankara, Turkey

July 23, 1944

Dear Family—

. . . I must be an awfully hearty thing—or do I mean hardy? Most everyone gets the upset stomach from the change of water, etc. but I am still all right. I'll knock on wood. Ellen has been unwell ever since we got here & did not feel well on the trip—with air sickness & everything. She has had a sore throat since we left Cairo & has been in bed with it the past two or three days, so I had to get another room—doctor's orders—so I wouldn't get it. . . .

I didn't get much sleep last night. Went to bed at 12:30 & up at 4:30 with bites—sand flies or bed bugs—I haven't determined but I stayed up & really got my clothes in shape. They charge 4 liras to wash & iron one dress so I'm doing my own. The lira is the Turkish dollar & equal to 55¢ in American money. Christina tried to tell me it was something that flew in the window & bit me & says I should sleep with the window closed. She believes that is much more healthful any way. It may have been sand flies but I'll find out for sure tonight. I looked for bugs but didn't find any. It was my first night in this bed. Christina says a pregnant Rumanian Princess had this room last week. Knowing that doesn't make up for bites though.

Had a very good time Friday night. Went to a dinner party—very informal. Supposed to have been four couples but Ellen couldn't go so another man came in her place. It was at a Turkish home where some of the Americans board—Madame Tuzond—or something like that is 35 years old, large, good looking, good natured & a wonderful cook. One of her daughters, a 14 year old, took a fancy to me & while we were sitting in the living room finishing our wine after dinner Madame came up to the Colonel and told him in French that her daughter wanted me to have a doll she had made in school. It's a lovely doll and was made very painstakingly & entirely by this girl. It's a Turkish dancing girl. Things like that can do me up—I was really affected by it. Anyway, I left the others & went out in the other room & struggled along in my awful French with Madame & four of her children & we had a fine time. . . .

After that we went to Karpiç's (pronounced Karpiches or Karpidges) for dancing. In my long letter you will hear more of that place—it's really something. If I haven't told you before, get the May 13th issue of the *Saturday Evening Post* & read there about it.[8] I wish you would cut out the article & send it to me. I haven't read it, just heard about it. There are many parties here & much dancing. The men are mostly good dancers too. The orchestras . . . are really very good & play all popular American music. Every night they play & sing "Peestil peckin' Mama." It's right across the street from the hotel where we are staying (Park Palas). . . .

Have been told that every bed in the country has bedbugs. Don't think it's that bad but it's generally accepted that there are a great many. I suppose you will have me fumigated before I enter your house next time—

Very buggy letter—Excuse it but they're on my mind as bedtime approaches. There are much worse things—like malaria mosquitoes—in other places, though, so I can't complain too much.

Best love to you,

Marge

✈ Ankara, Turkey

10 August 1944

Dear Mother—

Went on a tour last night that was very interesting. It was led by an archeologist—a woman and American too—who has been here since about 1932. We saw the ruins of old Roman baths, swimming pool, gymnasium. . . . Then up on the hill to see the ruins of a temple built in the year 10 A.D.

I was going home to write to you afterwards but the entire crowd was invited to Mr. and Mrs. Packers for waffles and I changed my mind and went along and I'm sure you will forgive me for not spending the evening writing because I enjoyed it so much.[9] The waffles were perfect—had American maple syrup, blackberry preserves, peach marmalade, apricot marmalade, real American coffee, marshmallows, American candy and canned fruit. We had cocktails first and olives, sweet pickles, pretzels and other American good stuff with them. We listened to the BBC and later the American news broadcast and after we were all stuffed with waffles and had relaxed for a bit had whiskey and soda and that is something you just can't get here. It was swell—super swell and I felt good. Not high—I don't mean. We drove home through the blackout, and it was my first experience at that. Mr. Packer brought us home and of course we all had to help look out for pedestrians, but it wasn't bad. . . .

We moved out of the hotel last Sunday and after a couple hours—we moved right back in again. The lady had not done all that she agreed to do and for other reasons we decided not to stay. When we went back to the hotel we took a different room (now I have been in four rooms in that hotel and have been on every floor) and the bugs have left me alone since then. Either they've taken the best from me or there are none in this room—anyway I can sleep straight through the night and that's all that matters to me.

The American girls here are awfully good about entertaining new girls. We were invited to lunch yesterday and the day before. And have had several other luncheon dates—either at apartments or at Karpiçs, but I'll tell you more about that another time. Tonight we are invited out for cocktails. . . .

I'm really suffering now for not having been a better correspondent because I don't get very much mail. I'm glad you write, Mother. I've had a letter from you in almost every pouch from Washington.

Best love to all of you,
Marge

✈ Ankara, Turkey
August 13, 1944
Dear Mother—
Have been living such a gay life—if this keeps up I should be a very different person when I finish my "tour of duty." The last three nights have been extra special—either fun or interesting—sometimes both. Thursday night went to a cocktail party. . . . They were all Americans at the party—most of them newcomers but altogether 20 or thirty people I suppose. A couple of them—one of them a career diplomat and almost the best looking young man I've ever seen and the Asst Commercial Attaché—Don Burton—asked me to join them for dinner. They were meeting another State Dept. fellow who just arrived that evening—Jeff Short—who is anything but short [and works in the Office of the Counselor for Economic Affairs]. Anyway I had dinner and dancing with all three of them at Karpiçs. . . .

The next night the Colonel [Theodore Babbitt, Assistant U.S. Military Attaché] had a party. The guests were mostly English—the other Americans. Can you imagine I wrote the place cards for the thing. It was my first encounter with the British—and the air was really thick with the veddy veddy British English. I have learned that I don't speak English. I speak American. It's very difficult not to acquire some of their habits of speech. We had cocktails at the Colonel's apartment &

then thru the blackout to Karpiçs. At dinner I sat between the British Air Vice Marshal and our [Brigadier] General [Richard Gentry] Tindall. Sounds impressive doesn't it—just so you will know it's your same old Margie—I'll make a confession—I used the wrong fork for my fish course. Apparently it wasn't too awful because the General asked me to a party last night. . . . We had a marvelous dinner as usual—I have never tasted such good consommé as Karpiçs have—and the white wine is the best I've ever tasted too. We had consommé chaud [for the] first course—then fish and white wine—then beef and vegetables with red wine—then a marvelous Karpiç concoction for dessert—it has cake, ice cream & custard in it & over all a high beautiful meringue. I have forgotten what they call it but it's delicious. The first time I had it was at my first American girls' luncheon (a weekly event). Then we had Turkish coffee & liqueur. . . .

Last night I was a substitute for Barbara Turner—one of the American girls here that I like especially. She had a toothache & could not go to the General's party so he asked me to help out. We had cocktails at the bar in Karpiçs till everyone had arrived—then to the table. It was so nice to be out in the garden again. It's the nicest place I know—it's always just right—never hot—sometimes a jacket feels very comfortable. There are never flies or mosquitoes & the sand flies seem to bite only in the daytime & at dusk so it's heavenly. The music is very good. They say that even in Istanbul there is no place that has better music. . . . I sat between the Czech minister [Dr. Milos Hanak] & [Naval] Commander [George C.] Miles—an American. The Polish M.A.[military attaché]—[Colonel Marian] Zimnal is very comical & lovable. Everyone likes him. His English is very funny—it's bad but is easily understood. Everyone laughs at things he says & he enjoys it as much as anyone. One of his favorite words is "approximately" & he uses it often. Another Polish man was with him & I don't know exactly how it happened but Zimnal asked me to a party Wednesday night & is calling for me himself—I wish I could remember the time he said he would call but I was so fascinated listening to the work he was making of it—I think it was minutes 15 before 9 or something. . . .

I do like it here. Have at last found office hours that suit me fine—go to work at 9:30, have lunch from 1:30 to 3:00, and quit at 7 o'clock and we never go out to dinner till 9 o'clock. . . .

I'm awfully glad that I came & I hope that you are too. I have been away from home as much as two years before so we should be able to do it again. I needed a change & I certainly got it. All of your letters are so cheerful. I hope you won't hold back if things aren't going well with you—take care of yourselves.

All my love,
Marge

⤜ Ankara, Turkey
14 August 1944
Dear Lillian—

. . . Will you please send me the recipe for coffee cake that is in my recipe box. It has cinnamon and sugar over the top and is dotted with butter—the coffee cake—not the recipe. Also your recipe for brownies. Chocolate and nuts are plentiful here and if we get into an apartment, it would be fun to have things like that.

Could you also send me some *nail polish* and *lipsticks*. I didn't bring enough of either and I don't believe that I have any in my trunk. Chen Yu, Revlon, Rubenstein, & Peggy Sage are all right in polishes. I like dry lipsticks but they're hard to find. Can't wear any purplish shades of either. I will also need more Kotex but not for a long time unless my trunk doesn't come. But use them in packing or to fill up the box anytime. Kleenex is all right too but I think I'll be able to get that from a nearer country. Anytime you want to put in a can of something that would suit me fine—I think of asparagus, tuna fish, mushrooms, Campbell's soup—however food is plentiful here. I haven't gained pounds but I have gained inches here. I just weighed this noon—53 kilos (2.2 pounds to the kilo). I don't get any exercise except dancing. At first I felt like protesting that I didn't dance but I gave that up long ago and now I just dance. I haven't found any man that was less than "fair" in dancing and some are very good. Anyway I have danced more in the last month—than in the past eight years put together. . . .

Incidentally I am going to send as much money home as I can but ask Duke to *send me a check book* so that if I get caught short I can draw a check. . . . I have to have money for income tax, and I want to help the folks but I also want some left over to set up an apartment for myself and a couple other dreams I'd like to realize when I return.

The last few days here have been so interesting but of course there are other days—and one has them wherever they are—when things do not look so *peki* (Turkish word for "all right" or "o.k."). Even on those days I don't regret coming but I do think longingly of a great many things at home.

Where is that letter a week? Did I tell you I played bridge in West Africa. And on the edge of the Sahara I drank Piney Point Specials (gin and grapefruit juice—the only other place I've had them was with the crowd at Piney Point, Maryland, where we named them) and watched a camel caravan go by. Shortly after, a slight sand storm blew up. Does it sound as strange to you as it does to me. To have seen the Amazon and the Nile, the Pyramids and had cocktails at Shepheard's in Cairo.[10] I wish I really had the capacity to make the most of all this but at any rate I enjoy it. I only wish I could pass it on for whatever its worth.

Best love,

Marge

Ankara, Turkey

August 17th [1944]

Dear Mother—

I think you've deserted me. The last letter I had from you was dated about July 10th. Ellen had a letter from her mother this week postmarked August 7th at New Jersey. I suppose your letters have been held up for some reason or just hit a slow pouch because I'm sure you've written. I hope you are all well and feel sure that you are. . . .

I'm enclosing a Karpiç list of yesterday's lunch with a rough translation in the margin that you probably won't even be able to read,—but you will see from that that we get plenty to eat.[11]

Had a fine time last night and must make a correction on my last letter. Zimnal—is Colonel Zimnal, the Polish Military Attaché. His assistant [Lt. Colonel Jan Rudnicki] whose last name I don't recall but I met at the previous party—first name is Jon, called Jonik (pronounced Yonik), the Scottish girl that was also at the party the other night and the Polish counselor—M. [Antoni ("Balo")] Balinski were there. Zimnal asked me to go on a picnic Sunday and I have a date with Monsieur Balinski (Antoni) for dinner Monday night. I like especially to dance with Balinski. Zimnoll kissed my hand after each dance with him and again when he said goodnight. They all three escorted me across the street to the hotel.

Haven't time to write more but I am well and within a week after you get this you should have the long letter that I've been trying to write for so long. Some that I have written to you will probably be repeated but I want to get it all together in readable form.

All my love to all of you,

Marge

Ankara, Turkey
August 23rd 1944
Dear Mother—

Just a note again. I can't write letters when there are people around. I will soon have a room to myself though so you can look for a long one. Ellen and I found a place last night where we can each have a room and will take all of our meals there too. We're moving Sunday. My room is a corner one where I will get the morning sun and there is a lovely view. It's in the flat of a Russian lady. The lady doesn't speak English but she speaks French. . . .

Will be so glad to get out of the hotel. I'm in good health but the bugs bother me terrifically. I have sandfly bites all over my arms and legs. The bedbugs visit about every other night. Their bites disappear but I always get up a couple times during the night searching for them after I'm bitten.

I'm enclosing a copy of that article I told you about that appeared in the *Saturday Evening Post*. It is a very accurate description of Ankara from all that I've seen and heard. Baba gave us white bread last night and the last time I had dinner there with Ellen he gave us black caviar—and it was very good. I didn't recognize it although I've tasted it before. It was spread on brown bread and it looked like burned cinnamon toast. Incidentally that white bread we had last night is the first I've seen in Turkey. It's always brown and made in the shape of a rye bread loaf at home. It's pretty good but doesn't taste like any kind of bread we have at home. Sometimes I get very hungry for some fresh white American bread—& stuff—

Have to cut this short—Be good—
All my love,
Marge

🜨 Ankara, Turkey
26 August 1944
Dearest Family—

I think you remember how happy I was in Washington when I worked for the Senator. Have talked about that ever since, but this has displaced it many times over. I have never had such fun, nor felt so good—both well and happy. The past three weeks I have stayed home only about three evenings and that was by choice because I turned down invitations. Every night it's parties—dinner and dancing. It sounds silly but I have to keep a date book. I've met a great many people. My favorites are three Poles and I love them. They are the most hospitable people and I always have a marvelous time with them. They are the Polish Military Attaché Colonel Zimnal (Marian—pronounced Mahreeyon), his assistant Colonel Rudowski (Janek—pronounced Yahnik) and the Polish counselor Monsieur Balinski (Antoni—pronounced as it looks of course). I could write at least a page on every evening. They are all very good dancers—but with Antoni I could dance forever—as Pat would say, "It's out of this world." Last night when we were dancing I understood him to say, "I would like to samba with you." I asked him to teach me—and he laughed and said, "Teach you—you are doing it now." So I guess he said I like instead of I would like. He is by far the best dancer here. I have never cared much for dancing and I know that I couldn't before—but here it seems to be a new discovery for me and I love it.

And I don't see how I can possibly have a trace of an inferiority complex left when I leave this place. I keep thinking the fun can't last and it will quiet down as it very well may when the war is over so I want to make the most of it while I can—and I know that it's good for me. I thrive on it and I'm happier than I've ever been in my life. The Poles have given me a great rush and they do such sweet things. Last Sunday I went on a picnic—and what a picnic—with Marian. We drove 90 kilometers (about 60 miles) to a very beautiful spot in the mountains. I could write an entire letter about that picnic—I have never been treated so royally in my life. It wasn't like a picnic at all. One day at lunch—my three were sitting together—and Marian sent his card over with the note "We have drunk just your health." His English is very funny—pronunciation is good but his grammar is awful and I wouldn't change it for the world. I don't see how he does it. They say that his French is the same way. "Just" and "approximately" are favorite words of his. One day he was explaining something and meant shortly before Attaturk died—but said "When Attaturk was approximately dead. . ." One night this week I went to dinner with Janek and Marian and when I came home from work to dress I received flowers from Antoni with a card saying "Thank you for the smile." He meant at lunch time. I had failed to see him one day and when he told me about it I told them that the next day I would be lunching there and I would make a special point of seeing him. You know things like that go to my head much more than wine—I feel almost giddy.

[Marge]

✈ Ankara, Turkey
  28 August 1944
  Dear Mother—

I can add just a note before the pouch closes. I got more flowers Saturday from Marian this time with a note to "Take care after yourself. It seems to me you are not well feeling and I am very sorry." I think he saw me at lunch time and thought I looked tired but I am very well. I will follow his advice though and I will stay home at least three nights a week. There are so many things to tell you about and I just don't have time but on these nights at home perhaps I can get caught up. . . .

Saturday night I went to dinner with a young Englishman—Peter Wainwright. I like him best of the English I have met. Sunday I was supposed to go on a picnic with Americans but I broke the date and slept late, washed clothes, did some mending, and enjoyed my flowers. Ellen went on the picnic and I so thoroughly enjoy being by myself. I had a wonderful time and at six o'clock went to a tea. It was a large affair and very nice. Mostly English and Americans but Marian was there too and he asked me if I would go for a walk in the car with him. I had promised to have dinner with Peter though and Marian insisted that all three of us go for a "walk in the car." Peter and Marian like each other and it's certainly a couple of extremes for me—after being around Marian for a while I feel that I'd better drop the French and start studying English grammar—but then with Peter I catch myself saying "really" and using the inflections they do in their speech. It's much fun. . . .

I do go out with several Americans, but I know Americans at home and over here it's sort of fun to learn something about others. . . . I have never lacked for friends among girls but I've never had men friends like this before and I think it's good for me.

I hope you are all well and that there will be some mail from you tomorrow. It takes so d— long for the mail.

Best love to all of you,

Marge

✈ Ankara, Turkey

31 August 1944

Dearest Family—

. . . Everything is still wonderful. Enjoyed Monday night very much with Balinski. You know I ate brain that night and liked it. With the Englishman Saturday night I ate a Russian dish that had chopped kidney in it and liked that too. Tuesday night I went to a party, . . . all Americans present. Last night I had to stay home because I wanted to stay home three nights this week—but it meant turning down a party given by Englishmen (I didn't want to go anyway) and also a dinner date with Short (I would have enjoyed). Saturday night my Polish friends are giving a party at the Embassy and both Ellen and I are invited. Sunday I will be with Marian and Monday night with Balinski again. That's a steady date for Monday nights and I hope nothing happens to stop it because I look forward so much to dancing with him.

I suppose you think it's crazy all this going around but I love it and I know it's good for me. I never go to any of these things without expecting to enjoy them and I always do—some much more than others—but I don't have that old dread and feeling of shyness that I used to have.

Last night I ate dinner in my room and practiced eating English style. It was sort of fun. They handle their knives and forks very efficiently and I feel so awkward forever switching my fork that I'd like to acquire at least that much of their customs. All the Europeans eat that way, and they pile all their food on the backs of their forks, using their knives—I don't like that so much, but I would like to eat fish and meat the way they do.

I went to bed very early last night and woke up when Ellen came in and we hashed over her evening. She was unusually late because it was a party in someone's home. Anyway I lay awake for awhile afterwards and heard the M— (I can't remember what he is called)—calling the people to prayer—from the Mosque in the old city.[12] His voice certainly carries in the quiet of the morning—about 4:30—and it was interesting and sort of pleasant to hear—sort of a musical chant. Short has been hearing it every morning and had called me on the telephone the night before so that I could hear but it was too late—he had just finished. . . .

Have to go—
All my love,
Marge

Ankara, Turkey
September 6th
Dearest Family—
. . . By now you have had a letter or two telling about the gay times. You know I never expected it to be quite like this & even if I had expected it—I would never have known how much I could enjoy it. It's perfectly wonderful. I like everyone & I'm having the time of my life—but I'm old enough not to lose my head about it. I don't know how permanent the changes are but certainly I have changed. For instance I simply can not sleep late in the morning & I seem to have ten times the energy I've ever had in my life.

The party at the Embassy Saturday night was fun—Balo (my "out of this world" dancer) called for Ellen & me & of course we rode in the embassy limousine with chauffeur—they all live—have apartments (or flats as they are called here) in the Embassy. We started at Marian's and Janek's. It was a small party—just the three favorites of mine. Balo, Janek, & Marian & Marian's dearest friend Major [Robert] Frick—the Swiss M.A.—two good looking South African girls—Ellen & me. We had drinks first then a buffet supper—that was marvelous—then over to Balo's flat for dancing. Their flats are very attractive & have unusually large rooms. The garden at the Embassy is the largest in Ankara & as it was a beautiful moonlit night (they all are beautiful but especially when there's a moon) we had to take a walk about the garden. We did not get home until two o'clock or after. Yet the next morning I couldn't sleep after 7:30 or so & got up & washed my hair & fooled around till Marian came at ten for the picnic. Janek had to work & couldn't go and Ellen didn't feel like going so it was just Marian & me again with food for four but we had a perfect day. I always enjoy being with him so much. He reminds Ellen of a big teddy bear. He likes me, I think, & we're always very comfortable in each other's company. He's never very serious—or serious for long—& he never gets romantic. He kisses my hand when we meet and when we say good bye. We drove south of Ankara this time & I'll tell you more some other time. . . . During the afternoon some Turk peasants came over. Marian gave them some of our fried chicken & some cigarettes—then they insisted on reciprocating by getting & giving us grapes. Then the word seemed to spread over the countryside because all afternoon they came with grapes for us— others we hadn't seen before—& we finally had to give money because we ran out of other things to give.

That night when I returned Short telephoned & asked me to go out for dinner so I showered & dressed & went out. I had turned him down once when he called last week so I didn't want to again & I had had such a restful & relaxing day anyway that I went out. I like him but we have such a completely different background for two Americans. He went to Harvard & traveled in Europe during summer vacations. Liked languages so often had private tutors & as a result speaks several languages fluently. He's only 31 years old, is 6 ft. 3 1/2 [inches] or more tall—very thin. He's the best tennis player here & plays every morning. He is extremely intelligent & from all that may sound stuffy or at least highhat but he isn't in the least. We had dinner at the Ankara Palas & then walked for miles—all over Ankara—& I mean miles—then we stopped at Karpiç's for wine & a couple of dances & then home. That's a slight variation on the usual evening—because it's always to Karpiç's for dinner & dancing until the place closes.

Monday night I had my weekly date for dinner & dancing with

Balo. He's a different sort of creature. I prefer being either with him or with Marian to anyone else in Ankara that I've met. . . .

I know you're interested in a lot of things besides my social life but the social life & the people are next to my heart. The Poles are so sweet & they always treat me so royally, it's fun. I can't help but like it. . . .

Do you know?—of course you don't—but my trunk came last week. When they told me my truck was at the Embassy & did I want it—I thought they were kidding. Some cologne spilled but didn't hurt anything & the tray was broken but nothing worse than that. That broke all records for anyone in Ankara because it didn't leave the States till July sometime. It seems that my life has taken a new turn—I've had such wonderful luck in everything since I started. . . .

There are a great many things to tell you about this place. I keep saying that & I suppose you are saying, "Well—give with some." It's a wonderful experience coming over here & I'm sure just "what the doctor ordered."

You must remember that I look at everything thru rose-colored glasses perhaps—it doesn't look the same to everyone. I can give you a realistic picture of as much as I've seen of the country—& I will honestly do that. . . . Mostly I'm interested in how differently I feel about things—& so deeply grateful for the change. . . .

I'm actually anxious for Ellen & me to get an apartment where we can entertain & return some of these parties. Incidentally I'm grateful for her—she's not moody & we get along uncommonly well—we've been together—traveling, working & living—since May 16th & there's never been a sour note in it. You know I don't think—or can't imagine walking into a party of strangers in Washington or even in Redfield with any shyness—the kind that makes you suffer—again. I've done it so many times here & not only lived through it but enjoyed it.

Love,
Marge

✈ Ankara, Turkey
September 7, 1944
Dear Kids (includes Dad, too),

Expect I'm disowned by this time—although I've had only one letter from each of you and I'm sure I've written at least three—and started countless others, as well. . . .

Before I get too far into this—I should dwell for a moment on some of the inconveniences here. The water is shut off every afternoon, generally off from about 1:30 until—& that's the worst—anywhere from 6:30 to 9:00 o'clock, then off again from midnight till about 6:30 in the morning. Sometimes when it comes on here at the hotel there is hot water only—& scalding at that. We run some in the tub & let it cool—which takes longer than you think when you're trying to be ready for an 8:30 date.

Number 2 are the bed bugs. They aren't actually in every bed in Turkey but almost—& some people they ignore—but I'm not one of those. I seem to draw them. And if you don't know what it is to awaken in the middle of the night with great welts itching great guns—realizing you're sleeping with the animals—searching & not being able to find them—you've never been in Turkey, that's all

Number 3 is the sand flies. Their bites itch too. I am not certain when they bite mostly but it seemed to be about 24 hours a day when I first came. I have become an expert on bites—bed bug bites disappear but sand fly bites stay—even after a couple of days—to scratch one of them it will swell & itch all over again—& for weeks there's a scar from each bite. My legs & arms have scars of dozens of bites but they have left me alone the past two weeks & the scars are beginning to disappear.

Number 4 is the blackout. I'm writing this by the light of one flickering candle & an overhead light of pale blue that might as well not be on at all. In fact there would be more sense in turning out the lights, throwing back the curtains & letting the moonlight stream in. It is really an art & I have it down to a system now of coming home—laying out my clothes, purse & everything I need while I can still see, then stewing around if the water isn't on—calling the desk & they helpfully send up a couple pint bottles of water—then putting on makeup with the aid of candle light & a flash light [that] a pilot recently insisted upon giving us. Then down to the lobby into full glaring lights where we face our date & wonder if we put rouge on one side & not the other. . . .

Number 5 is gyppy tummy. But I can't complain about that—but 9 out of 10 who come here—or even more that get it & continue to. A few have had sand fly fever too & it's something like certain types of malaria. The gyppy tummy is stomach pains & a great deal of time spent in the bathroom—& what bathrooms! There are other diseases too but so far I haven't had anything. Have never felt better in my life. I can't even sleep mornings & I feel especially good when I've been out carousing the night before. I haven't been drinking a whole lot—but one night—I reviewed it the next day & could hardly believe it—but had gin & vermouth cocktails—white & red wine with dinner—vodka—peppermint frappe (crème de menthe) & ended up with Canadian whisky—& I felt perfectly swell the next day.

Number 6 is the City itself. It leaves much to be desired. Istanbul, for instance, would be far more interesting. Ankara is not large (population 120,000) & except for the citadel or the "old city" on the hill is not very picturesque. They say that Istanbul is beautiful.

Number 7—the people. When one goes to a foreign country—they expect to make friends among the citizens of that country but it's almost impossible here. As a result the foreigners sort of band together—& the result is something like a small town—like living in a goldfish bowl. Everyone goes to the same places—Karpiçs—95% till now. A couple night clubs are opening now for the winter so that should spread the foreigners out a bit. Anyway everyone knows everyone else's business & talks about it freely.

Number 8 is the language barrier. I wish I could speak at least French fluently. . . .

Now I feel better that I've said all that & when you've finished deciphering this please send it to my folks to read. Now be sure because I feel guilty I've written such glowing accounts to them. The truth is I never think of the things that are unpleasant. Except when I'm forced to—like bedbugs for instance—they can be quite forceful.

I can't think of any more disagreeable things but I'm sure that Ellen could if I asked her.

[Marge]

→ Ankara, Turkey
7 September 1944
Dear Lillian—

I'm enclosing some scraps that I've written now and then. I don't have time to rewrite them. I'm sure they will give both you and the censor a headache.[13] Hope it won't delay the whole letter. . . .

The letters I've written are a mess but perhaps you get the general idea of what it's like living here—and can you blame me for loving it. It reminds me so much of the way I felt that year in Washington—and like Washington, I'm wondering if I would be able to recapture it if I left and then returned. I doubt it, but what I want to do now is return to the States at the end of my two years and then go out to a new place if I can. Everyone, as I've repeated so many times, doesn't like it so much as I do—but I've been fortunate in the people who have been nice to me and that makes all the difference in the world. I keep thinking it can't last—that I will like it so much—but something nice is always happening and it keeps me on top of the world.

Have to go—
Love to all of you, Marge

* * *

. . .The Turkish toilet is very simple—two slightly raised foot rests and a drain. Also there are sometimes thick wooden clogs for those who don't wear shoes. Our bathroom at the hotel is just like one you might find in any small town hotel in the States. All the bathrooms I have seen have showers built over the tubs but I have yet to see a shower curtain and as a result when we have finished our showers there's a lot of water on the floor, but under the tub where we have outlet pipes there is a drain and the water just falls out of the tub and down the drain.

* * *

All the dinners I've been to the past week were at Karpiçs, where we eat in the garden at night. It is one of the loveliest spots I've ever been in—Ankara would be a cold and dismal place without it and sweet Baba Karpiç is the very heart of it. He is well known even outside of Turkey. Several articles have been written about him and published in American magazines. . . .

Many languages are spoken but especially Turkish, of course, and

French—with either, one can get along—but I know at least one is a necessity. My two years of high school French has helped but so little—it's hardly worth mentioning and my accent is very bad.

* * *

I expected the summer to be hot here but it isn't—in fact it's the most delightful climate I've ever known, and why anyone leaves Ankara to go to Istanbul for the summer, I cannot understand. Every day the sun shines, sometimes there is a slight breeze but never windy. The mornings and evenings are cool—generally one needs to wear a jacket in the evening. It is warm during the day but never uncomfortably warm. Eating at Karpiç's at night is perfect—no wind, no flies or mosquitoes, always stars—sometimes a moon. I overheard someone asking one of the Poles how he had been and he said that he had been suffering from the heat the past few days—I nearly fell off my chair. Because there is boating and swimming at Istanbul, they seem to think that is the only bearable place to spend a summer in Turkey. They admit, however, that the climate is muggy there. I am anxious to see Istanbul—I've heard so much about it. It's not such a long trip—seems like going to Minneapolis from Redfield or New York from Washington. If I can't make it before November though I shall probably wait until next summer because summer is definitely the time to go and the winters are terrifically cold.

* * *

Although we came by air, it took us 26 days from the day we left Washington, so we had a few days at various stops along the way and I was grateful for the delays because we always managed to get off the base into town. It was interesting and we had some crazy experiences. It really doesn't seem possible that one Marjorie has actually seen the places she has—like the jungles, the Amazon, African bush country, the Sahara, the Nile, the pyramids and Cairo. I only wish she had the capacity and the background to thoroughly appreciate and absorb it all. Had rather looked forward to making the last stretch of the trip on the famous Taurus Express but we did not. We came up in a Turkish plane but that was fun too. It was small compared to the planes we had been riding in—held only six passengers—and we bobbed around some and sort of hedgehopped over the mountains. I have seen the Taurus though—it's one of the things people sort of do socially here—

go down to see someone off, and it really looks like the perfect setting for mystery stories.[14]

Haven't seen much of Turkey yet—except Ankara and Ankara is so unlike the rest of the country that it seems almost false. So bear in mind that what I write of Ankara [is] not typical of Turkey. Almost everyone wears western clothes—it's difficult for me to distinguish nationalities—and Attaturk Boulevard could easily be a street in an American city. The Boulevard is heavily lined with trees and shrubbery but beyond it on the hills is what is called the "Old City" and there's scarcely a tree in sight. The old city has never failed to impress me as a backdrop. It doesn't look real and from a distance it looks clean and the colors are rather soft and attractive. It is only when you get into it and walk around that it looks old and not so clean—but after seeing Cairo and other places—Ankara looks clean even in its dirtiest spots. The Turks don't stare and I've rarely seen a beggar here.

The cost of living here is terrific. Food is plentiful but very expensive. The fruits are wonderful here. The season for oranges was over when we arrived but we have had figs, oranges, pears, peaches, grapes, apples, all delicious. I like the apricots especially and the melons are the best I've ever tasted. One kind is very much like our honey dew and they also have watermelons that are very red and very sweet. Nuts are comparatively cheap here and very good—I will at last get my fill of hazel nuts and almonds and they serve pistachio nuts at the bars the way our bars serve popcorn.

* * *

Whisky can be had but the price is so high that no one drinks it. I think it's six or seven liras a drink. Votka and gin are the most popular. A quart of votka is seven liras. I rather like it but I couldn't say what it tastes like—it doesn't seem to have any taste and it looks like water. I think the reason I like it is that it mystifies me that anything so innocent looking and tasting could be so potent and I certainly recommend extreme caution to beginners. The white wine is especially good. I like the red wine too. I don't like the cognac. Beer is good here. Had a crazy experience last night. The native fire water is raki. It smells and tastes strongly of anise and I don't care for it. It is clear and colorless, until water is added, then it looks like diluted milk.

In true Turkish cooking everything is cooked in mutton grease. I am not at all anxious to try it. Places where we eat like Karpiç's, the Gar (similar to Karpiç's), and the Ankara Palas do not cook in mutton grease.

✈ Ankara, Turkey
15 September 1944
Dearest Family—
I boasted about my health a little early, but I'm still lucky I've had nothing serious. . . . I've had nothing worse than a bad throat so it's nothing to be concerned about and there's plenty of sulfa available. I had the throat last week and responded so quickly to sulfa that I was well & back at work in no time—too soon I guess because I got it again this week & am taking it easier this time. Of course, being sick was just an excuse for more flowers and callers & I've had a fine time. . . .

Monday night I had my regular date with Balo. Tuesday night Ellen and I were invited for cocktails to the French Embassy. The Vichy French were obliged to move out a short time ago so our friends moved in.[15] The night before I got sick last week we met the Secretary of the French Embassy so the invitation was the result. It's the most beautiful Embassy in Ankara and they took us all through it. Tapestries, chandeliers, and everything are gorgeous. They have a swimming pool too—the only Embassy that has [one]. Everyone has been telling me since what a hit I made with M. [Charles] Lucet, the Secretary—that he wants to ask me to dinner. . . .

[Marge]

✈ Ankara, Turkey
21 September 1944
Dear Family—
. . .The weather has gotten much cooler. Along with colder weather they say the social life picks up. Can't see how there's room for it to pick up much—except I guess the parties get larger and evening dresses are worn often. Balo is having a party next week that will be my first dress-up party in Ankara. Feel mighty subdued today because I went to a big party last night at the French Embassy. It's a beautiful place. Have been there once before—it was last week—and at that time they took us all over the place. . . . Last night's party was sort of a housewarming—it

was the First Secretary's first party in his new quarters. I'll call him Charles—because I guess I might as well get used to calling him that anyway. It was a large cocktail party and I was obliged to go alone—as I was invited alone and of course it's perfectly all right. I was the only American girl there—in fact there were only about three other Americans there. One of them was my boss—the General. Had my hand kissed every time I turned around but I'm getting quite accustomed to it—that's what I get for having a "Mrs." in front of my name. Charles asked me to have dinner with him after the party and I accepted; then he included Balo and the daughter of the Swiss Ambassador—so the four of us went to Serge's for dinner and dancing. Francoise is only 20 and said I had to be her chaperon. The three of them are very good friends and enjoyed the evening very much. Charles wanted to know if he could take me to dinner some night soon and from other reports— I am told that I have been adopted by another foreigner. I don't understand it—why my success if you want to call it that?—but it is fun.

Must get to work.

Best love,

Marge

✈ Ankara, Turkey

25 September 1944

Dearest Family—

. . . Working through lunch today so that I can leave at 5:30 instead of 7:00 tonight. I'm supposed to be at the Polish Embassy at 8:00 and I am not even sure of what I will wear. I'm a little nervous about it because Balo likes my clothes and thinks I have very good taste. This will be the first time I've worn a long dress and I hope it will be all right. He is having the party for an English woman—a friend of his—who is an artist, and is leaving Ankara. I haven't met her but saw one of her paintings at the French Embassy. Of course I'm impressed and then Balo confided that he intended to have all the best looking women in Ankara at the party so naturally I'm scared and will probably look my worst.

I'll write tomorrow night.

Much love,

Marge

✈ Ankara, Turkey
Sept. 26, 1944
Dear Lillian—

… I have your letter and I'm going to try to answer some of the questions. Stayed home tonight and washed my hair and washed clothes & fixed my nails. Mail came in today but not a scrap for me. I never seem to be able to write more than to the family & I really suffer for it when the mail comes in. . . .

There are about 20 American girls here in Ankara now I believe. I wish I could describe living here to you so that you could really see it. . . .

Ankara is full of "characters" and I do mean characters. Ellen and I can't figure out why there are so many in one place—unless everyone just gets that way when they've been here for a time. I don't know what to call them except characters—but they are sort of odd—or rather so many have such individual personalities—they are completely different from anyone else. I could write pages of thumbnail sketches—but I'm afraid I couldn't make you see them even then. Ellen thinks Steinbach is one & I know she is one so perhaps we're a little that way too. Although we agree we sort of like the "odd" ones—at any rate we certainly enjoy them—gives us much reason for laughing.

You know I rave on so about all this—it's because I like being here so much. I may get tired of it—I'm not sure—I know I don't want to stay in Turkey more than two years, but I don't mind that—the two years I mean. I do work too you know—even though I talk about everything else but work. There are a number of things that aren't pleasant I suppose, but I never think of them & they don't bother me. . . . I have hinted before that everyone doesn't feel the way . . . I do. Ellen is the one. I'm so glad that of the two of us it wasn't I. She has resigned and will be back in the States before Christmas. I hate to have her go and I'll miss her very much. . . .

It's 12:30 & I haven't gone halfway through your letter.
Much love,
Marge

⇥ Ankara, Turkey
26 September 1944
Dear Family—
Have a few minutes so I'll start this here and finish it when I get to the hotel.

The party was fun. It was much smaller than I had expected. Balo certainly had an assortment—most parties have about two men for every girl but not Balo. I suspect him of wishing he could surround himself with them—girls I mean. Anyway the party was just four men and four girls. The girls were one English (the artist), one Swiss (Francoise), one Scottish, and one American (yours truly). The men were one Pole (Balo), one French (Charles), one Greek, and one Englishman (the artist's husband). Everyone spoke English. I'm going to dinner with Charles tomorrow night, to lunch with the Greek Thursday noon, and dinner with Balo Thursday night—since we didn't have our regular Monday night date. Incidentally, my dress was all right. I wore dress by Sally [Norbeck], earrings by Dorothy, and fur jacket by Vera. I certainly have reminders of all my friends with me at all times. Evening mitts by Sally too. We had cocktails at Balo's first. Then to Serge's for dinner and dancing. The dinner was especially good. Balo knows how to order, and I'm beginning to think the food at Serge's is better than Karpiç's. Had crepe suzettes for dessert—the second time I've had them. . . .

Loads of love,
Marge
September 29, 1944
[P.S.] I am wondering if you worry that I'll wear myself out going out so much. I feel much better when I do go out—not so nervous & I don't get in stews & I feel very happy—I get more sleep than I did in Washington because we don't have to be at work until 9:30 & I'm always in bed by about one o'clock—everything closes between 12:30 & 1:00 & we never go out until 8:30 or 9:00 (unless it's an early cocktail party). Americans could learn a lot from the foreigners' way of living. They think food is very important & believe that Americans don't appreciate food—I could write much about that—but one thing I've learned to like especially is drinking wine with dinner.

Incidentally, I like my work & the fellow I work with is very difficult but I think he's beginning to believe I'm all right, so everything is good—

✈ Ankara, Turkey
14 October 1944
Dear Mother—

Two letters from you yesterday—postmarked 14th and 22nd of September—all about pheasants. After reading them, I just stared out the window for about fifteen minutes day dreaming and wishing I could drop in for a pheasant dinner and some hunting too. Is it easier to get shells this year?[16] Ten a day is a terrific number. Hunting must be wonderful....

I was going to stay home every night for two weeks—made that announcement last week to the friends but it didn't last long because too many things were doing—so it has been the same as others and I've had one night at home. Went on a hike last Sunday—which for me and a few others was mostly a jeep ride rather than a hike. We were in three groups of about five each and took different routes to the top of a mountain where we met and ate and returned, mixing up the groups and taking different routes on the way back. We had a Turk, a Pole, one Swiss, one French, Americans and English, and one Russian. We started in the morning but it was nine o'clock that night before we got back to Ankara and then we went up to [American Embassy attaché G. Huntington] Hunt Damon's for drinks and hot soup—those who had come back in the jeep were about frozen. Saturday night I went to a long dress party at Whitman's—one of the American Embassy secretaries. It was a good party—one other American girl present besides the Ambassador's daughter [Dulci Ann].[17] There was a mixture of everyone—all nationalities—and I love parties like that....

Tuesday night I went to another good party at Hunt Damon's.... The party was mostly Americans but was given for the Iraqian minister who left this week and his wife.... Ellen wasn't there but the Iraqian knows her and told me that Ellen and I look something alike. We don't but I explained that we were both of Norwegian descent and perhaps that was the reason he thought so.... A Swiss told Ellen that we don't look like the other American girls.... Actually they all—or most—have a queer idea about Americans formed from movies [and] the new rich American travelers to some extent at least. Lucet who has lived in Washington and Balo who has lived in New York don't think I'm so different. . . . Wednesday night I met Balo at Serge's for cocktails after work. Then we had supper there and afterwards went to his place at the Embassy, listened to the radio, played records, talked about poetry believe it or not. Haven't danced with him for almost two weeks because they are observing a period of mourning for those who were killed in Warsaw.[18] . . .

Sally wrote that this was such a good spot & I think it is too but perhaps in a different way than I had expected to. Europeans think it is awful but I think it's interesting. In Ankara you could almost imagine you were in a town in the States—people do not dress so differently—most of them—but as soon as you get into the country it's completely different. Sunday we stopped in so many villages to ask directions to find the road that would get us closest to the mountain we wanted to climb, and at each place I thought it would be a good idea to take the census—because the whole village would turn out and gather around the jeep. There they always wear the old costumes of baggy trousers—generally patched till you can't tell what the original material was—the women wear quite colorful things. I want to get some pictures of them, and especially of the carts drawn by oxen and of these huge sheep dogs that look ferocious—and of threshing the grain by hand. They spread out something like a big blanket, and all the grain is piled on that—looks like gold in the sun & so clean & neat looking the way it is heaped on the big blanket then they pull the blanket up & sew it into a bag with the grain in it, load it onto a two-wheeled cart that is drawn by oxen & it looks & sounds like the heaviest thing in the world to pull. The carts often have solid wooden wheels—there are pictures of them in that *Geographic* I sent to you before I left, & they squeak & squawk with every inch—when there are five or six of them straining & squeaking down the road together it's really something to hear. The veil is supposed to be taboo but not all the women in the country have discarded them.

The peasants are friendly & pleasant as they generally are the world over. One village that we stopped in—they were bringing in grapes—I've never tasted any so wonderful as the grapes here & especially if they've just been picked. As soon as we stopped they brought out a plate & put huge clusters of grapes on it, washed them & brought them to us. We offered money but they wouldn't take any. At this same place we saw them pressing grapes—with bare feet. We drove the jeep to a village right at the foot of the mountain—in fact those villagers call it their mountain—& left it there. We got a donkey to carry the stuff—food & coats—to the top & started up. The view was marvelous—miles & miles of hills & mountains—not many trees but colorful from mineral deposits I guess—we weren't very far from the village when the [muezzin] came out on the roof of one of the flat topped huts of the village to call the people to prayer—that chant always fascinates me—I love it!

[Marge]

✈ Ankara, Turkey

18 November 1944

Dear Pat—

...Ellen is leaving soon and I gave a luncheon for her today—a small one of six girls—those that Ellen likes best. I am so sorry to have her leave but perhaps it is better for her. It has taken a long time to know her but I am so fond of her—I'm getting soft in my old age I guess. I know I'm going to cry when that plane takes off....

Our two new girls have been here a couple of weeks & the older one is like an answer to a prayer. She spent the summer in the States (Little Rock is home) and before that worked in the M.A. office in Mexico City. It's like a paradise there. That might be a good spot for my next assignment except that there are rarely any vacancies there. The two new girls are Corelli Jernigan and Virginia Sipp. Corelli is the older and I know we'll get on well together. I mean I think....

Did I tell you about going to a movie here? I've tried it once but don't know when I'll get up the courage to try again. It was Don Ameche & Joan Bennett or someone that looked like her in *Girl Crazy* or *Girl* [*Trouble*] something. Anyway I went with Ellen one Sunday afternoon. Have to buy tickets in advance because they sell out. As it was we couldn't sit together. I had to climb over a lot of people to get to my seat—so I felt obliged to stay there in spite of the sensation of things crawling on me and an occasional bite. They always have intermission half way thru the feature. I had just begun to get interested in the picture—was good to see an American film again—first since Cairo—when intermission came. By that time I had gotten myself in control—so that I could ignore the desire to scratch everyplace at once—& was actually enjoying the show but at intermission when Ellen saw the welts on my legs she wouldn't hear of it & insisted on leaving at once. . . .

Haven't seen the election returns yet—all of them I mean—& I'm anxious to. On election night Balo took Jeff Short, Francoise & me to dinner at Serge's. Afterwards at about one a.m. we were invited to a party at [assistant United States military attaché] Captain [Walter Ewart] Seager's & General Tindall's to hear the returns. We knew it was quite hopeless to hear much till later that morning,[19] but it was fun anyway and I finally met the Ambassador [Steinhardt]. . . . There was only one other girl besides Francoise & me so it was really a men's party but it was rather a quiet & serious one because everyone was hoping for news. They had a special broadcast & I got a thrill out of hearing the announcer say, in describing the momentous evening so important & of such great interest to all the world, that the American Ambassador was at General Tindall's house with other friends listening to the radio—& I thought gosh—I'm here too—that's us! Then sometime later [assistant United States military attaché] Colonel [Theodore] Babbitt took me home & someone asked if we would give so & so a lift—we did & so & so turned out to be the radio announcer who had described the great evening sometime earlier. He had come to the General's too after introducing the short wave broadcast from America. . . .

Have been going on walks almost every Sunday—Balo & Lucet are always quite insistent about it. Last Sunday I called Balo to say I wouldn't come—I spent about 5 minutes explaining & assuring him that I wouldn't change my mind—thought he was all convinced & he said, "Your excuse is not good enough, we will fetch you in 20 minutes, be ready, goodbye."

The walkers were all meeting at the Polish Embassy—then Balo fairly pushed Lucet out the door to "fetch" me so I went. We walked more than 12 miles. I was supposed to have gone to a tea late that afternoon & a party after that, but when we returned I was too tired to dress for the tea so had tea at the Polish Embassy with the others. Came home to dress for the party & was too tired so went to bed. The walk was good for me though & have done enough so that I had no stiffness or soreness as a result. The places where I have walked are very beautiful—not like those barren hills in the back of the pictures I sent. They're much higher—very few trees—but colorful in spite of it. . . .

The weather is beginning to change but I still think it's the most wonderful climate I've ever known—I'm afraid I'm going to be more particular about the climate in which I live after this. . . .

I haven't sent any Christmas packages home to you and I feel awfully guilty about it, but there isn't anything that I could get that couldn't be had at home—much nicer for half the price—so it will have to be money instead. . . .

Take care of yourself, Pat, and keep good and happy.

Much love,

Marge

Ankara, Turkey

23 November 1944

Dearest Family—

Wondering what you are doing this Thanksgiving Day. Dinner at Lillian's or dinner at Mother's? At Lillian's I suppose, and Mother bringing pies and things from home.

I packed my things at the hotel this morning and tomorrow morning they will be moved to the room that Ellen has vacated. Had lunch with Corelli at Karpiç's. Afterwards there was a football game at the stadium (touch football) between the military "Redskins" and the Embassy "Palefaces," but it was called off at the half on account of rain. It is raining today and it's really a grey day but not unpleasant. It snowed some a few days ago—not in the low part of Ankara, but on the higher parts. The mountains are covered with snow. Hope there will be a lot of snow this winter, it's nice and makes me think of South Dakota. The climate is actually a lot like South Dakota's climate at its best. I love the cold clear days but they haven't been really cold yet. Tonight all the Americans go to the Steinhardt's for a buffet supper—turkey, cranberries, pumpkin pie, and all the rest that goes with an American Thanksgiving dinner. There will be a movie too and dancing I think and hope. It is the custom on all American holidays to go to the Steinhardt's. I suppose that is the only time I will ever go there.

[Marge]

Ankara, Turkey
5 December 1944
Dearest Mother—

. . . I moved into Ellen's room when she left. It sounds crazy but I'm living with a Chinese and his Swiss housekeeper. I have tea & orange juice for breakfast. Mlle. Muller, the housekeeper, is a darling always smiling. She keeps the place immaculate & takes very good care of me. I know she's an excellent cook but so far haven't had any meals because the few times I've been home I haven't wanted to eat. I am charged only for the meals that I eat so it won't be so expensive. My room is 100 liras a month & will pay extra for my laundry. It will probably be 200 liras a month altogether which is very reasonable for Ankara.

You asked about church and movies. There are Catholic services in some of the Embassies but there are no churches. Mlle. Muller and I were talking about it the other day. She misses the church bells so much. We will have holly and mistletoe and Christmas decorations everywhere. Last Sunday I didn't go on the walk, but Balo came here after the walk with an armful of the most beautiful mistletoe. It was the first that I knew it grew around here. I've never seen such beautiful mistletoe. Mlle. Muller arranged it in my room, over all the pictures & everywhere. I went to the movies that night with Balo, Francoise & Jeff. It was *Angels with Dirty Faces* with the Dead End Kids & I stayed thru the show without getting a single bite so I'm glad it can be done. Although I'll only go rarely because I don't want to carry bugs home on my clothes. Mlle. Muller almost never goes to movies just for that reason. . . .

Tomorrow night I'm having dinner with Colonel B[abbitt]. He is a wonderful dancer—really the best in Ankara—& he thinks I dance well—that's the only attraction. He is a lot of fun though & I don't think anyone is so enthusiastically liked by everyone who meets him. Thursday night dinner with Balo, Friday night home, Saturday lunch

& shopping with Balo. Balo is forever giving me little things that he picks up, so he's promised to show me the places & perhaps I can find some things. He brought me a silver snuff box from Istanbul and when I moved into this room he gave me a little Turkish dish with a cover. I found out from Mlle. Muller that it's for ink. It has a lovely design on it. He gave me a piece of Damascus brocade about 12 inches square, and a small Turkish table scarf embroidered with gold & stuff. Mlle. Muller says they are very expensive. . . .

I think I have some very good friends here. Was just thinking they are all "best" of something or other. I like them all so much and hate to know that after these two years I'll probably never see any of them again, but it's nice to know them. . . .

[Marge]

🕊 Ankara, Turkey
18 December 1944
Dearest Family—
With luck you should get this by New Years or there abouts. Hope you had a wonderful Christmas. I'm sure we will have a good one here—at least as good as it can be. . . .

Stayed home every night for a week because I thought it would be good for me, but I don't enjoy being alone too much. I read five books during that time and of course had no cocktails or wine. Should have written a lot of letters but didn't feel in the mood for that. Yesterday we were to go on a walk and I had my lunch all ready but it had been raining for a couple of days and I didn't feel like walking in the mud so I brought the lunch that Mlle. Muller had prepared for me to the office and shared with some of the GIs, then played cribbage with them the rest of the afternoon. Listened to the radio for awhile after that—tried to get an American broadcast . . . but the best I could do was a BBC broadcast of American recordings—made me a little homesick, . . . then I went home and read another book. Probably the week at home did me some good, but I feel happier and better when I'm going out.

Love,
Marjorie

✈ Ankara, Turkey.
26 December 1944
Dearest Family—

How was your Christmas? Happy I hope. Mine was fine. Like any kid I must tell you about my gifts first—a lovely bracelet of red coral and silver, a basket of flowers, two boxes of candy, perfume, a silver match box, handkerchiefs, a cut glass perfume bottle, a scarf, American cigarettes, and two bottles of Scotch. Scotch is practically priceless here. . . .

Christmas Eve we went to the Ambassador's. It was the same as Thanksgiving but the atmosphere seemed different. First we saw a movie—Cary Grant in *Mr. Lucky* and a community sing with words on the screen. Then downstairs again for hors d'oeuvres and scotch and champagne. The table—about 30 ft. long at least—was loaded with food and I'm going to list just the things I can remember but there was a lot more—turkey, ham, lobster, fish, beef, sweet potatoes, corn on the cob, baked beans, scalloped mushrooms, scalloped corn, cranberries, chestnuts, olives, pickled onions, etc., cauliflower, white biscuits, fruit salad, potato salad, vegetable salad, and for dessert had fruit jello with whipped cream, chocolate crème, apple pie, mince pie, lemon tarts, orange cake, plum pudding, fruit cake, chocolate éclairs and so on and so on. There was lots more and always great quantities of food left. I hadn't eaten all day but I certainly made up for several days and I had four or five desserts. And of course the scotch and champagne were excellent. After everyone was stuffed Santa Claus came and there were gifts for everyone—all the girls received either a scarf or stockings and six packages of American cigarettes, the men got socks and cigarettes, the officers a bottle of champagne and cigarettes. They really do it up on a grand and generous scale. We had dancing of course and I had a dance with the Ambassador much to my surprise. Colonel Babbitt took me home. . . .

Last night I had a date with Balo and I always enjoy my dates with him. We went to Serge's as we always do and ate (again!) and danced. The place was 80 percent English and Americans and the holiday mood made it much gayer and noisier than usual—and Americans make any place noisier. . . .

Have to go—
All my love,
Marjorie

→ Ankara, Turkey
26 December 1944
Dear All Seven of You,

I'm absolutely speechless. Your Christmas packages came today. They tried to get me to open them at the office but I thought there might be K[otex] in there so I brought them home and have just opened them & tried on everything possible (except the K) to try on and I can't get over it. You sent me much too much & I didn't intend for you to try to send anything. . . . The cigarettes—you really shouldn't have. I know how hard they are to get. I always run out before my next ration comes around but then I can smoke Turkish cigarettes—not too good but not too bad. . . .

I hope you all had a wonderful Christmas. I was thinking the other day that the last Christmas I had in Redfield was 1937. . . .

Don't feel much like going to a party tonight but I can't let down some friends. Some of the Army at Serge's last night had the orchestra playing "Margie" about every third number. Then a couple of them wanted me to dance. I didn't because I was with Balo, but promised I'd dance with them tonight at the USO party.[20] They are nice fellows and I don't want to do anything to make them dislike me.

I am leaving my Chinese and Swiss and moving to an apartment on Jan. 15th. Barbara Turner has the apartment and Corelli and I are moving in with her. It will be nicer in many ways but I've liked my Swiss lady and been content here except for the hot water. Miss Muller heats the water on the stove the nights there isn't any in the tap but we have a hot water heater at the apartment. . . .

It was so much fun to open the packages from home. The boxes weren't broken at all. I got a thrill out of thinking of you wrapping the things and putting them in—then they travelled such a long way & I was the next one to touch them. . . .

All my love,
Marge

→ Ankara, Turkey
4 January 1945
Dearest Dorothy,

Have to tell you about New Years before it grows dim. There had been a party every night for two weeks before—but there's a party almost every night the year round for that matter. At any rate it had been more strenuous than usual but in spite of it I promised to get up for a picnic on Sunday, last day of '44, to start at 9:30. We had expected to have a station wagon and were going to drive some 100 kilometers south of Ankara to a river where it is traditional to throw in a kurus [Turkish coin] and make a wish on the last day of the year. Ewart had arranged it with great pains the day before—and because we generally take walks (once it was a thirteen-mile walk) on Sundays, I kept referring to it as a walk and each time he corrected me saying there would be precious little walking. So instead of wearing slacks and the usual hiking outfit, I wore a suit and coat, no hat, or scarf, but at least I wore flat-heeled shoes. As it turned out everything went wrong the first half of the day. Ewart overslept, we couldn't have the station wagon, etc., etc. So instead of starting at 9:30 in the station wagon for a beautiful drive through the snow covered countryside—we left at 11:30 in a jeep—7 of us—Ewart, Barbara [Turner, an embassy co-worker], Jeff, Francoise, Milo Talbot,[21] Balo, and I. I wanted to back out and go home and go to bed because I had been at a late party the night before but they wouldn't hear of it. I protested every step of the way until we started and then everything was all right for me but everyone was embarrassingly solicitous of my comfort. The worst was that I didn't have boots on because we had to walk in snow and mud. It was a perfect day—clear and not too cold. The mountains looked beautiful and it reminded those who have been in Switzerland of the scenery there, except the mountains are not so high. Whenever we drive in the country—we are always pursued by huge sheep dogs from time to time. I've never seen any dogs like them—they are the size of great Danes but heavier slightly—generally a pale yellow color—and because they are so large and strong, seem very vicious and I guess they are. . . .

The jeep was acting peculiarly and we wondered if the day was jinxed and if we would ever get back to Ankara that day. We walked for a very short distance and it was decided that it was too cold to eat outdoors and [my] feet were too wet so we went into a Turkish village—one of the smallest—to see if we could go into someone's home to warm up and have our lunch. It was necessary to remove our shoes before entering and we went into a room about the size of your dining room. There was no furniture in it but on two sides the wall jutted out to form a low and wide bench, which was covered with Turkish rugs. The floor was covered with light-colored rugs that looked rather like Indian blankets but with very little design. In the center of the room was a small stove in which they built a roaring fire. The village had a population of 150 people and there were 6 persons to a house so the head man from each house must have been in that room with us because I counted 25. We all sat around the sides, either cross-legged or at least with our feet up, and the men filed past and each one shook hands with each of us and said we were welcome. It was charming. Then they all sat on the floor cross-legged. We passed around cigarettes to them and of course they all smoked and we all smoked. The room was packed with people, the fire was roaring, and the windows were nailed shut. For a time it looked like the foreigners (don't forget that's us) were doing a strip act because we kept shedding more clothes. Soon they brought coffee in and the unheard of thing was that they served the coffee to the women first. In the conversation we learned that one of the men from the village was a *kavass* (sort of messenger, chauffeur, doorman, janitor or anything else) at the British Embassy and we deduced that he had probably informed the villagers of the strange ways of foreigners—of serving women first.

When the door opened to admit more villagers for the show we saw women in their gaily colored dresses—and many veiled—hovering around the door and working in the next room. Jeff thought they were making bread and asked permission to see them, so one of the men took him to another building and he came back and reported the great activities that were going on. All the women were hurrying around preparing dinner for us. We held a quick consultation and of course there was only one thing to do, we must eat their food and give them ours, which we did of course, and the only thing we didn't give them were the ham sandwiches, which of course would be an insult to them.

First they brought a low table, which I am sure should have been placed on the floor and we would sit cross-legged around it, but they fixed it up in front of us so the table top was on a level with our feet—which was worse than having it slightly above the level of our feet on the floor because the result was that everytime someone moved or shifted his position, he would invariably get his foot in the food—especially the bread, which was the first thing brought to the table and serves as napkin, and bread. The bread looked like Scandinavian flat bread but was not stiff and it was brought in great folds about two feet long and five inches wide. Folds of bread circled the table and on that they indiscriminately scattered seven large spoons and seven forks. The first dish served was chicken—chunks of chicken in broth in a dish like a large aluminum soup plate. That was put in the center of the table—as were all the others and everyone dipped. We were glad to share the same dish—after all Jeff who is 6 ft. 4" and hollow from head to toe was with us and our hosts wouldn't notice how little we ate. Then we had yort [yogurt], and a dish of soup, and a grape compote and a couple other dishes of stuff. We gave them our food but mostly they just watched us and talked to us. I'm sure they must have thought our manners were awful, but they seemed to enjoy the visit and they were certainly hospitable.

We got back at about five o'clock in the afternoon and went to Jeff's for rum and tea. Then home and Ewart asked me to join some of them for dinner but I was afraid I couldn't make it because I had too much to do. At any rate I dressed and went to [an] eggnog party at 6:30. Intended to leave a few minutes after 7:00 but . . . the Ambassador joined us and I didn't think it was proper to walk out of the presence of His Excellency so I stayed and stayed, but finally when a couple more people joined our conversation, I slipped out. And really rushed home and dressed up in that dress of yours I nearly wore out trying on before I left last summer—the one with the tails. It was the first white-tie party I'd been invited to. I wore your earrings and Corelli's rhinestone bracelet, and a small clip of jet and diamonds belonging to Mlle. Muller. Milorad called for me at 8:30 and we went out in the "120 horse" (Yugoslav Embassy Cadillac)—out to Penna's.

After some cocktails there we proceeded to the Hanak's (The Czech Minister) for the biggest event of the season.[22] All the diplomats were there and the crowd really glittered. It was not so gay as it should have been because there were too many people and the program was too long. It was a concert ending with a sketch at midnight. After that there was dancing, roulette, bridge, liquor and food. We stayed for awhile and then decided to move on to smaller parties. Had intended to make the rounds of the best and the worst night spots in Ankara and end up with private parties, but we didn't get very far and ended up at Ewarts where I for one found all the people I like best so settled down there. Got home at about seven in the morning. It was a wonderful way to spend the last day of '44 and the first part of '45. Sunday morning to Monday morning seemed at least a week long it was so full. Have had some wonderful times. Some of the best have been impromptu like the night before Ellen left when we didn't go to bed at all but after a very elegant breakfast of pancakes and champagne took her to the airport.

[Marge]

✈ Ankara, Turkey
11 January 1945
Dearest Family—

Just a note again but I'm staying at home tonight so I hope to do something about that but mostly I expect to sleep. I really have a home now too. Sharing a place with Corelli and Barbara Turner. It's the first floor of a house. No central heating but there are three wood stoves and it's been very comfortably warm. What is more important than central heating is a hot water heater and we do have that so we have hot showers or baths whenever we want them. There are two bedrooms and Corelli and I are in one that has twin beds. We have one servant who does everything. She is Greek and her name is Sultana. I like both Barbara and Corelli and I hope we will get along well. . . .

Have had a letter from Ellen and I guess she is happy to be home. . . . I hope she will be happy but I love being here. People say that when you begin to like Ankara, then be careful because there's something wrong with you—but I don't believe it. I've liked it almost ever since I got here and I feel more "right" than I ever have in my life. . . .

Have to work.
Much, much love,
Marge

✈ Ankara, Turkey
January 15, 1945
Dearest Mother—

. . . I like my new home very much. We're going to have one of the fellows from the office come up for lunch someday and take pictures of us all over the house and of the maid and everything to send home.

Corelli and I are going to Palestine for a week—leaving either the 23rd or the 29th.[23] . . . It's just decided that we're leaving on the 23rd by plane and returning on the 29th and we're getting very excited about it. I'll write all about it when I come back of course. . . .

All my love,
Marge

✈ Ankara, Turkey
5 February 1945
Dearest Family—

I wonder if I'll ever catch up with things to tell you and ask, etc., etc., before I come home. It doesn't seem that I ever will. . . .

This is not an attempt to catch up. I just have a few minutes before quitting time and nothing to do at the moment—not really time to collect my thoughts and tell you about the trip as it should be done but briefly. I loved Jerusalem, Beirut and Damascus. They are beautiful cities and much more interesting than Ankara. Got such a thrill out of the olive trees, orange groves, lemons, tangerines, and grapefruit groves. It isn't the right time of the year for olives but all the citrus trees were laden with fruit and I've never tasted such wonderful oranges. They all looked like Christmas trees—such a rich green and heavy with bright-colored fruit—from yellow lemons to the deep orange of tangerines. On the bus from Tel Aviv to Jerusalem, Corelli and I were talking of fruits and canning as though we were on a bus in Washington going down Connecticut Avenue and I asked her if our conversation didn't strike her as odd when we looked about at the people in the bus and considered where we were. I'm sure it's beautiful country at any time but coming from the snow and barrenness of Turkey we appreciated it much more. The trip down was extra special—it was such a beautiful day and now I ride in the planes with such complete confidence that I was sorry it was such a short trip.

[Marge]

>| Ankara, Turkey
12 February 1945
Dearest Family—
Spent a wonderful lazy Sunday at home yesterday. . . . I went thru all my letters and read and burned all of them. 95 percent were from Mother and it was almost as good as a day at home. I mean at home in South Dakota.

I'm enclosing a copy of a letter I started more than a month ago to Dorothy. Enjoyed that day and night so much—but the best part of it was having lunch in the village—it was so unexpected. . . .

Have something on every night this week. Wish I had time to write about everything but don't have time even for a diary. My engagement book will be my memory book I guess. . . .

The dry cleaning problem is very bad here—for one thing it costs TL 7.00 for a dress or a suit. One gold colored dress cost TL 10.00 (or $5.53). And the cleaning is hard on the clothes. So if Lillian could pick up things with that in mind it would be a help. . . . If she [could send] a couple of summer dresses—and don't get office type because I can wear any old thing to the office—but dresses for cocktail parties.

Oh darn. I'm having complications with my dates for tonight. It's a headache. . . . My regular date with Balo is tonight and the pilot—Sammy—from Cairo is here just for this one evening. He just telephoned so I'll see him at 6:00 and Balo at 8:00. Damn! . . .

Much love,
[Marge]

>| Ankara, Turkey
21 February 1945
Dearest Lillian—
. . . Am staying at the office through lunch today. Crazy notion I have but I can't write a personal letter unless I'm alone. . . .

I'm still going out as much as ever. Spasmodically I say I'm going to

stay home more but I never do. I enjoy going out so I suppose I'll continue as long as people will have me. I'm seeing Balo off for Istanbul on
the Taurus at 6:00 o'clock. At 8:00 I'm going to dinner with Colonel
Babbitt and at 10:30 we're going to a farewell party for Mr. Steinhardt.[24]
Tomorrow night we go to the Steinhardt's for cocktails at 6:30 and afterwards to a party at Ewart's for his brother, Colonel Cedric Seager,
who will be down from [the American consulate in] Istanbul.... Even
though I go out with others and have fun and love being here—I dread
to think of what it will be like if Balo should leave. We recently celebrated our 25th anniversary—25 Monday nights and there have been
countless others in between. He is marvelous. In all the times we have
been together we never run out of things to talk about and I guess he
knows all my family and friends and my whole life as well as I know
his. He's the kindest and most unselfish person I know—and that's
not just my opinion. He has a very clever wit and is always making me
laugh.... Last week one night we had a wonderful time—most unusual
evening—we thought it would be pleasant to spend an evening reading. It may sound crazy but you have no idea how I enjoyed it. We had
stacks of reading material and I had my latest *Time* magazines (which
are coming through wonderfully). We had cocktails and sandwiches at
our elbows and just read and talked, listened to BBC, and about 9:30
the cook brought in a whole platterful of Polish pancakes that I love.
Have often had them at picnics and loved them cold, but these were
hot and freshly made—I ate six. They are like crepe suzettes (thin pancakes, you know) only bigger and rolled around spiced ground beef.
Now of course I'm rambling. It wasn't necessary to tell you all that but
so many people ask his advice on things—especially of the heart—that
I told him I thought he needed some advice—and that he would be
wiser to treat me with more indifference—then maybe I'd pursue him
for a change. He said, "No," he's not trying any techniques on me (and
I know it—he's really a darling)....

Must get to work now—just wanted to give your imagination
something to work on. I have sometimes hesitated elaborating on a
lot of things or writing as I really feel about them. I don't want to ever
make you restless or feel that you have missed something—this kind
of living is artificial you know but it was just what I needed. Someday
I'll have memories and look what you will have—Jack and Sally and

grandchildren.[25] Oh well—in ten years I'll probably be back in Washington beating a typewriter.

Best love,
Marge

✈ Ankara, Turkey
March 12, 1945
Dearest Mother—
This [thirty-first] birthday is certainly different from any other I've ever had. Saturday night Balo and Charles called for me looking very beautiful in white ties and tails. From there we went to Hunt Damon's for a buffet supper and after that to a ball—a charity thing and many people in Old Turkish costumes. After that Francoise, Jeff, the Princess [Victoreeya or Victorilla of Romania], Charles, and Balo and I went to Balo's and drank whisky. The next day, Sunday, yesterday (seems years ago), had intended to go for a walk with Balo but at noon Colonel Babbitt telephoned and asked if he might come over with a contribution for our liquor supply. He came, then Balo and as it was cold and very windy we gave up the idea of a walk and Corelli, Colonel Babbitt, Balo, and I shared a picnic lunch intended for two.

At six thirty Balo, Colonel Babbitt and I went to the movies, *Fanny by Gaslight*—odd name—a British picture and quite good. When we came out of there at 8:30 or 9:00 there was a blizzard raging and we were very hungry so we went to Karpiç for food. Another man—very good friend of ours—joined us at the bar and later asked us to have a drink with him and his friends at Serge's. It was a terrific night and someday I can tell you all about it. I'll certainly never forget it—for many reasons. We finished the night at Serge drinking champagne and dancing at three o'clock this morning. Had six men on my hands and was toasted so many times, and so many compliments—I know it made me giddy. Balo and Ted brought me home. I invited them in for a drink and to talk over the events of the evening. We had no sooner than gotten in when the telephone rang and our host telephoned to tell me goodnight. It's really too much, Mother—it's like living a charmed life since I've been here and one day I expect a terrific blow and I will come down to earth again. Honestly, I'm not flirting—I know the girls around here probably think I'm a—I'm not sure what. I just love being here and so many people have been so nice to me. Several—and I do mean several—men have very respectfully told me—awfully extravagant things. It really is a new experience for me and it's too much, that's all I have to say about it. . . .

Tonight I have my usual Monday night date with Balo. Last time Balo went to Istanbul he brought me the most interesting and good looking pin—very old and made of silver with red coral stones—matches the very beautiful bracelet he gave me for Christmas. He also brought my birthday present which was two very lovely silver cups or goblets—can use them for cigarettes or flowers. He's always buying things for me and he's like a child about them—couldn't wait until my birthday to show them to me, but was so anxious to know if I liked them that he had to give them to me at once.

I write so many things about parties and frivolous things I may give a wrong impression. My work is not bad—although I should prefer another boss—we get along all right most of the time and as far as being aware of the war—I may not write about it but I certainly am very conscious of it—and last night more than any other time but will tell you about that another time. . . .

Have to go out and the pouch is closing.

Loads of love to all of you,

Marge

→ Ankara, Turkey

7 April 1945

Dear Lillian—

. . . Easter [1 April] was especially nice—started early in the morning; declined a breakfast party, went to the airport with Balo, Ted and Corelli to see the Ambassador off; then to Catholic services at the chapel in the Italian Legation; then votka and sausages at the Polish Embassy (Polish Easter custom); lunch at Karpiç's; two-hour walk with Ted and Balo; tea and Easter music at Balo's; an hour's nap; dinner and dancing with Ted.

Easter Monday we had to play a joke on Balo. Got up bright and early and—perhaps I'd better tell you [the] custom. Balo told us that on Easter Monday—anytime before noon—you may pour water on anyone you want to. Where there are many children in the house—of course the place is drenched before noon—but no one can scold. Of course, we thought he had practically invited it so Ted and I went out to Balo's. Balo came to the door and was too sleepy and astonished to see us at that hour to realize what was happening. It was a sight anyway and I wish I had a camera. It was fun and Balo loved it too—as all the Poles did when he told them about it. . . .

Perhaps if I were unhappy here, everyone would be awfully good about writing but of course you all know I'm not. It's so funny too—guess I'm crazy—because no one, or almost no one, else enjoys it so much as I do. One of the officers wrote home after he got here and said that this is a harsh and unlovely country, inhabited by a harsh and unlovely people, speaking a harsh and unlovely language. In spite of that and although I know I'll never return, I feel awfully warm and happy here and I'll always think of Ankara with pleasure.

There are a lot of things I'd like to write about but I'm restraining myself. Are the no letters a sign of disapproval?

Much love,

Marge

✈ Ankara, Turkey

20 April 1945

Dear Mother—

We had a wonderful time on Corelli's birthday. Virginia [Sipp], Corelli and I had lunch at Karpiç—something we've always wanted to have—just caviar, salad and glacé souffle (baked Alaska). It was wonderful and Balo brought a bottle of champagne—and we had a birthday cake too. . . . The Prime Minister—Saraçoğlu—spoke to us when he came in, bowed again when he left. We had the table next to his & he was amused by our party.[26] . . .

Charles' birthday was this week too. It came on Monday. Balo wanted to give a lunch for him, but Charles said only if it was small and he selected the guests. It was just Charles, Victorilla, Balo, and I. Victorilla is the Princess you know—but she's not a snob. She's young, about 27, attractive, vivacious, but kind and a good friend. Had a very good lunch, but you should have seen the birthday cake. It was a tremendous thing and had candles larger than the kind we used to use on the Christmas tree—and 55 of them. I'm sure the fire raised the temperature at Karpiç's several degrees. Charles was only 35, but Balo said he told Baba that he didn't know how old Charles was so just put on as many candles as you think he looks. We gave him a little silver cup. Balo and Victorilla bought it. . . .

Have a letter started to you someplace about the news of the President's death & will enclose it.[27] Went to a service at our Embassy on Saturday morning. All the diplomats were there in uniform or morning suits. My Poles looked nice—Marian (Col. Zimnal) in uniform with his shoulder weighted down with a whole lot of medals, Balo in top hat, cutaway coat & striped trousers. . . . Still my favorite people in Ankara.

Sometimes I should really just send a list of names & nicknames with a brief sketch on each one so you would know these people too—there are a lot of interesting people here.

[Marge]

⤴ Ankara, Turkey
  10 May 1945[28]
  Dear Dad and Mother—
  . . . Our month of mourning is almost over—ends at sundown this Saturday. It's been awkward with the celebrations this week. Of course we're not celebrating [V-E Day, 8 May 1945] but the British have been both officially and privately and the Russians put a big sign on the Embassy with the word "Victory" (in Russian of course) in blue lights and they celebrated all night Tuesday. Of course it's good that poor old tired Europe can rest and recuperate and I'm happy that it's over but couldn't feel very elated about the news—suppose it's because the war in the Pacific is still going on.

It happened that on Monday some officers were here from Cairo and invited us to a party that night, so we celebrated in a way. Went to [assistant United States military attaché] Colonel [Frederick A.] Pillet's for cocktails and then fifteen of us—eleven were officers—went on to Karpiç for dinner and what a dinner. It was simply out of this world. Caviar, lobster, chateaubriand, fresh strawberries and whipped cream. Then we returned to Colonel Pillet's for dancing. It was altogether a very nice party—but the dinner was the high point. Dear old Baba presented me with the caviar—and I really helped myself a plenty. Ted said he thought he saw Baba wince as I dug in. It was his gift to us and it costs about 70 liras a kilo at least—or around $20.00 a pound—roughly. Baba is very pleased with the way I've turned out—he used to fuss so because he didn't think I ate enough and at first I didn't like caviar too much—but now I'm a fanatic on it and Baba just grins at me and makes motions and puffs his cheeks to tell me I'm getting fat. Think I'd better look around for a transfer to someplace where the food isn't so good to get back my "figger."

Balo is coming in on the plane from Cairo and Ted, Corelli, and I are going out to meet him. He sent me a cable last week saying he hoped that I was having a good rest far from Europe and Africa—at that time Ted was in Istanbul. I did have a rest for three days but then Ted came back and have been with him every evening and two or three times for lunch. Ted goes back to Istanbul today but Balo will be here, so that's the way it goes. It's fun though. They are both so much fun....

Guess I'd better get to work.

Much love and take care of yourselves,

Marge

✈ Ankara, Turkey

14 May 1945

Dear Dad and Mother—

No mail at all for me in the last pouch—hope that means there will certainly be something this pouch.

The weather is summer-like now. Not wearing a coat any more but haven't gone into summer dresses yet. There wasn't much in-between weather—just winter to summer....

Tomorrow will complete one year of my contract so next year at this time I'll be wending my way home. The heaviest demobilization should be out of the way by that time so may be able to choose my route home as well as the method of travel. Hope so. It would be fun to have a cruise down the Mediterranean and visit a couple other countries on the way. Spring fever really has me—I'm day dreaming now and must get to work.

Best love,

Marge

⤴ Ankara, Turkey

28 May 1945

Dear Dad and Mother—

The other box came. Don't know whether I told you or not. The one with the Kleenex, hand cream, tuna fish, and coffee. Corelli and I had the tuna fish for lunch immediately and it was wonderful. The sachet powder was a nice surprise. Am using it and like it very much.

Hope there will be some mail today.

Our new boss [Ambassador Edwin C. Wilson] came and seems awfully nice. Took him only 50 hours from Washington to Cairo. Makes it seem only a short distance home but of course that's what a star will do for one. . . .

Must get to work.

Love,

Marge

⤴ Ankara, Turkey

11 June 1945

Dear Dad and Mother—

. . . Having a big party this week. The M.A. [military attaché] and his assistants are having all the M.A.'s for dinner—taking over Serge's Thursday night this week. Had expected to have it at the Tennis Club, but the evenings are too cool and the weather not dependable at the moment and the Tennis Club would be outside dining and dancing. Wrote invitations for 116 people and we're not getting many regrets so there will be close to a hundred there—and that's really too many for Serge's. There will be only 13 Americans in that group—seven American officers, our new Ambassador who just arrived—Ambassador Wilson and his wife who is Hungarian and her mother—and Corelli, Virginia, and I. Actually only 11 Americans since the Ambassador's wife and mother-in-law are Hungarian. . . .

Haven't spent an evening at home for two weeks but expect to stay home tomorrow evening unless there is a moon—in which case there will be a moonlight picnic. The climate is awfully nice—as I've told you before. Went on a picnic yesterday—Charles, Balo, Ted, Corelli, and I. Went to an awfully nice spot near the little village that we visited December 31st—when the people in the village prepared food for us. . . .

Please send me two more boxes of Adrienne face powder. Be sure the shade is Rachel Olive. Just discovered that one of the boxes Lillian sent me is another shade and much too light. . . .

Best love to all of you,

Marge

P.S. There's an article on Turkey in the May *National Geographic* you might be interested in reading. Haven't had time to read it yet but have seen the pictures and they're good but don't care for the photographer's selection of things to photograph. Was here at the time Mr. Williams was—last fall—but didn't know him although I remember seeing him. Someone said he's written about Turkey in a way that makes you think it's a paradise. Most of the people here will disagree with him I'm afraid.[29]

✈ Ankara, Turkey

14 June 1945

Dear Dad and Mother—

. . . This is the day of the big party and we're all just about standing on our heads. Like a dummy it didn't occur to me that uniform and decorations meant white tie for those without uniforms. Discovered quite by accident while discussing the party with Colonel Babbitt. The party is being given at Serge's instead of at the Tennis Club so it will be dining and dancing indoors. The party will take over the Paviyyon [pavilion] of course and no one else will be admitted. Out of the 113, 77 are coming. And we're all relieved. Each time a "regret" came in we thanked Allah because the most Serge's has ever had in his place was 96 and it was much too many. He said best not more than 80 so we're nicely under. There will be 51 men and 26 ladies—about half are Turkish, the rest American, British, Chinese, Russian, Greek, French, Swiss, Norwegian, Polish, and Yugoslav. I'm going to have Marian (the Polish Military Attaché), on my right, a Turkish officer that I don't know—Binbaşi Örge—on my left. Across from me will be Colonel Frick who is the Swiss Military Attaché and Marian's bosom friend. Also at the table will be the Spanish Military Attaché and wife, the Norwegian Military Attaché (Colonel Hans Holstad), the new Turkish Military Attaché to Washington, Binbaşi Alpkartal, who is leaving for the States soon, the wives of two Turkish officers—Bayan Tolgay and Bayan Tulga—and the niece of Binbaşi Örge—Bayan Gökart—and an American officer, Major Hanst from Texas who is a bore. I'm very pleased but did my best to finagle a seat next to Marian and with Colonel Frick at the same table. It should be fun.

Balo's name date was yesterday. [It will] take some doing to explain "name dates" but in European countries, at least among Catholics, the birthday is celebrated quietly by the family and best friends don't know when it is—just because the anniversary of the christening, which is the patron saint's day, is made much over—that is the "name day." Anyway had lunch with him and last night the Ambassador and the Polish Embassy staff had a party for him.

Was going to stay home Tuesday night and go out dancing with Ted Wednesday night, but Ted had to go to the new American Ambassador's for dinner last night so we changed our date to Tuesday. Then Wednesday all the officers and Corelli, Virginia and I were invited out to [Edward B.] Lawson's (the American Commercial Attaché and the two most loved people in Ankara) for cocktails as a farewell party for Colonel Babbitt who is going to Istanbul to stay. He will return for a day or two from time to time but mostly I've lost my best dancing partner. Balo is both pleased and sorry because he sincerely likes Ted but there is a little conflict at times when I have a date with one and the other one wants to go out too. Like both of them very much. . . .

Balo is going to Istanbul—leaving next Tuesday and returning the following Monday morning. Looks like a very quiet week for this person. Balo and Ted both think it's funny. Some people have an odd sense of humor. . . .

Must go. Hope there will be a million letters for me today.

Best love,

Marge

→ Ankara, Turkey
18 June 1945
Dear Dad and Mother—
At last the absence of mail has been explained. Today received the fourth pouch—possibly fifth—in which I have had no mail, not even *Time* magazines. Someone along the line got the bright idea that we

were Embassy employees and therefore not entitled to use the APO address and they have apparently been returning our mail to the states. ... We *are* entitled to use the APO and would have a beautiful lynching if we could get our hands on the person who has been withholding or returning our mail.

Haven't time to write a long letter but will try to have a long one in the next pouch. The party was a great success and I had a marvelous time. Am sure my table was the best. Had a long visit with Colonel Holstad, the Norwegian Military Attaché, and he's a sweetheart. He's 67 years old and is returning to Norway in a few days where he will return to his retired status. He was very interested in me as an American of Norwegian descent, and told Colonel Zimnal that I looked so Norwegian that he believed I could have come directly from Oslo.... The Turkish officer on my left knew about as many words in English as I do in Turkish but he had a twinkle in his eye and we got along very well. He called the office twice afterwards—once to say what a good time he had and the second time to say what a good time his wife had. Anyway I was thanked. Of course Colonel Zimnal, the Polish M.A., was on my right and that guaranteed that I would have a good time— and Colonel Frick across from me is an old friend too. Obviously there were no Russians at my table.[30] It was daylight when I went to bed— the second time that has happened to me in Turkey. The other was the night before Ellen left.[31] We were among the last to leave the party— felt rather obliged to stay that late because the party was given by the M.A. and his Assistants. We were not obliged but did stop at the Ass't Navel Attaché's apartment for a nightcap and then to our place where we fried eggs and watched the sun come up. The sunrises are almost as beautiful as the sunsets but probably the only way I'll ever see them will be to stay up that late....

Had a marvelous day yesterday. Balo and I had a wonderful walk in the afternoon—out in the country thru a beautiful valley. Balo loves to walk and does every Sunday. I like to walk all right but find it almost impossible to climb—get so out of breadth and my heart pounds. Yesterday Balo chose a very good one with not too much climbing. We walked fast for three hours with not more than thirty minutes out to sit in the shade and so I could smoke a cigarette. I was exhausted afterwards but after a hot bath and a cocktail felt completely refreshed, and we went to the garden at Karpitch's for dinner and dancing. Went home early.

Should have gone to Istanbul when I had a chance, I've learned to my sorrow. Now private secretary to the General and the job is no joke. He works very much like the Senator did—and I'm enjoying it but it keeps me on my toes. . . .

Much love,
Marge

✈ Ankara, Turkey
20 June 1945
Dear Dad and Mother—

While I have a chance I guess I'd better get off a letter to you for the pouch tomorrow. . . . We're all so unhappy about the mail situation and we're not looking for any mail for sometime—we think it may be three, four or five weeks before we will get any. . . .

Had lunch with Balo and Colonel Zimnal yesterday and afterwards took Balo to the plane. We were there in time—at least the plane hadn't gone yet—but they didn't let Balo on but gave him a ticket for today. . . . We went through the same routine today but got him off this time. . . . While Balo was arranging for his luggage I talked with an American lieutenant—very young—who was there with several other young American officers. Hadn't said very much to him when he said, "I'm surprised that you speak English, so few people around here do." Don't suppose I should have told him that I was an American because it embarrassed him. . . . When I came back and told Corelli . . . she said that it is high time that I'm going back to the States, when people start taking me for a foreigner it's proof that I've been here too long. . . .

Just thinking it's been a year today since I've had a glass of honest-to-goodness milk and I swear I don't think I'll have any teeth left when I come back. No one is afflicted with pink toothbrush here—but with red toothbrush.[32] Someone has said that it's a vitamin deficiency. Have always thought it strange that the vegetables are so tasteless here. Fruits are wonderful but the vegetables are flat. . . .

Have always meant to tell you about the ironing boards here. They don't exist. Ironing is done on a flat table. Sultana recently acquired a sleeve board so I guess she has a life of ease now compared with others. Our Warrant Officer's wife—who has never been in America—is so proud of an English ironing board that she has. It's a board—collapsible, folds in the center, why, I don't know—that she rests on the table and the other end on the top of a chair.

The brooms are funny. They are like outsize whisk brooms with no more handle than whiskbrooms have. There is very little wood in Turkey but even so ironing boards and broom handles would be so helpful—but no one seems to think of making things easier for women here.

And the kitchens—I've told you about them before. The kitchen utensils are practically nil—no mixing bowls and about three or four kettles—a stove with two or three burners—usually no oven. But the amazing thing is the quantity and quality of things the cooks can prepare—and the variety—from a kitchen like that. The most I've even tried to do is fry eggs—I do that better than Sultana but Corelli and I don't think our cook is any good and we eat no meals there. Haven't done anything in a kitchen actually since I left home and then I didn't do much.

All my love,
Marge

Ankara, Turkey
25 June 1945
Dearest Family—

. . . Balo is returning from Istanbul on the plane this morning and I'm having lunch with him. Looking forward to talking with him again. . . .

Balo has done more to make my stay in Ankara happy than anyone or anything. For months he has telephoned every morning—because he likes to—and because it's such an easy way for me to get up in the morning. Never mind answering the telephone but hate to be fussed at or use an alarm clock. Anyway the telephoning works very well. When Balo went to Istanbul he said that his spirit would stay in Ankara. Didn't know what he meant till the next morning and the next and every morning that he has been gone I've had a phone call every morning at 8:30 sharp. Haven't the faintest notion who it is because they never say a word—just hang up after I've answered. Balo has telephoned a couple of times from Istanbul and yesterday—I told him I couldn't understand it, have awakened each morning at 8:30 sharp and haven't used the alarm clock at all. He laughed and said it must be his spirit. The telephoning is only an example of how sweet he is. He's fun.

Must go now. If I have time will write more before the pouch closes but I can't think today.

Love to everyone,
Marge

✈ Ankara, Turkey
26 June 1945
Dear Dad and Mother—
. . . Balo came back yesterday and instead of having lunch with him alone, had lunch with three of my favorite people—Balo, Marian, and Charles. Charles had just received orders to leave Ankara—and he is leaving on Tuesday's plane for Paris. I'm sure I'll never see him again in Turkey—but hope to see him again in Paris or Washington, and somehow I think I will. He was expecting to leave but not before the middle or last of July and the notice is much too short, but a couple of parties have been planned already. We're awfully unhappy to have him leave—and he's unhappy too. Guess we'll probably all cry at the airport on Tuesday. Wanted everything to stay just as it has been and it keeps changing all the time. . . .

27 June 1945
. . . Corelli and I went down to Karpitch for lunch today and in addition to the lunch we ordered we received the following from Baba— all on the house of course—first corn on the cob, then caviar (a whole tin of it), then fresh tomatoes, cucumbers, and pickles. . . .

Shouldn't make you unhappy by telling you all about the food here, but you know we'd trade it all for a coke or a milk shake and a sandwich at the corner drug.

The weather here is absolutely sublime. Summers couldn't possibly be nicer. The winter wasn't so awful, but most houses were kind of cold, whether they had central heating or not. Most evenings I wasn't at home except to change or to sleep and I guess I didn't notice the cold so much. But whenever anyone says anything about whether the winters are cold, Corelli sort of moans and says, "No one will know what I suffered." Have heard that so many times and always laughed but I know she minded it terribly. . . .

Have work to do—
Love to everyone,
Marge

>{ Ankara, Turkey
14 August 1945
Dear Dad and Mother—

Never have time to write any more. But I'm well and happy as ever. Used to write during office hours but I'm almost earning my salary again now and like it very much.

Corelli and I are going to Istanbul for the weekend—leaving Friday night, returning Monday morning. It's like going to Mpls [Minneapolis] for the weekend as it's an all night trip on the train both ways— leaving at 6:15, arriving at 9:00 next morning each way. So it's a lot of traveling for a short visit but think it will be fun and the next time my boss goes away I will go down there for longer. Balo is going to put us on the train and instead of flowers, said he would be practical and give us Polish pancakes, wine and fruit. . . .

Aren't the atomic bombs the most fantastic thing—sounds like something out of Buck Rogers comic strip.[33] Everyone's been talking about them since the first news of them. On Friday when we heard the news of the first peace overtures we all got so excited. The office was fun all afternoon and the General [Tindall] quickly arranged a small cocktail party for that night. We went to that and afterwards to Karpitch's for dinner and every last American was there that night I guess. We are hoping each day to hear that the fighting has stopped and that the war is really over.[34]

All my love,
Marge

⊁ Ankara, Turkey

20 Aug. 1945

Dear Lillian—

Just got back from Istanbul this morning and had lunch with Balo and the Polish Consul General from Istanbul. The Turks recognized the new Polish Government today so it means that all of my friends among them—the Government-in-Exile Poles—will probably be leaving very soon. . . .

This noon [Balo] gave me some good luck pieces for Jack and Sally [Enstrom]. I'm enclosing them—there are four—the two really old ones are either Roman or Greek—Balo and Rudowski argued about which they were—but anyway the smaller one is for Jack because of the horse on it—the other with the head (which they decided looks like the Polish Minister in Cairo) is for Sally and the other two are Turkish coins believed [to be from] Atatürk's time although not very recent because they weren't yet using modern lettering. . . . [Balo] won't be here much longer. As soon as he gets his visa, which certainly won't be long now, he will arrange for transportation and then go to the States. . . .

I'll write you about the Istanbul trip another time. I'm well and happy.

Best love,

Margie

⊁ Ankara, Turkey

21 Aug. 1945

Dear Lillian,

Balo has just been here for drinks and gone on to a dinner party— I'm spending the evening writing. . . . Because [Balo is] leaving soon, he has started cleaning out things and tonight brought me a huge globular crystal vase—suitable for gold fish—punch bowl—or flowers that I've always admired. . . .

Must get on with the other letters.

Much love,

Margie

[P.S.] Istanbul is fantastic—the beauties of the Bosporus are impossible to describe but Ankara is home to me and I prefer being here. Will tell you about the other another time or when I come home. My visit was too short to really form a conclusive opinion about whether or not I'd like working there. . . .

🖂 Ankara, Turkey
10 September 1945
Dear Dad and Mother—
Back in Ankara again after a perfectly marvelous vacation in Istanbul for nearly two weeks. . . .

Summer is over almost but the weather is still very warm. It was perfect in Istanbul and I got a suntan. Balo was there at the same time and I was out with either Balo or Ted all the time and sometimes with both. Will write you all about it but the pouch is closing now.

Best love to all of you,
Marge

🖂 Ankara, Turkey
8 October 1945
Dear Dad and Mother—
The big news arrived in the last pouch—on the 4th and I sent the cable to you that day. I'm enclosing a letter for Mr. and Mrs. Du. Please address it for me and send it on to them. I feel like a grandmother now that Pat's married. Guess it would be more right if I should feel like an old spinster. Now that it's done I think it's perfectly swell—Pat's and Du's marrying, I mean.[35] They are young in years of course but maybe it's a good thing—and there's no doubt that they are very much in love and Du is so nice and they both have good sense. . . .

Just seven months and seven days of the two-year contract left. Balo is waiting for his visa to America, then he will arrange for transportation. The State Department [is] so slow, but apparently everything is in order now and he should get it before too long.

Congressman Karl Mundt was here last week. Don't know whether I wrote to you about him or not. Had been expecting him here for a couple of weeks but he was in the hospital down at Cairo with amoebic dysentery. He came up in a special plane with Congresswoman Bolton from Ohio. It was fun to talk with him about South Dakota and should have liked more time to hear about his trip.[36] I talked with him for only about fifteen minutes or so. He looked well and the people who met him here seemed to like him. I wonder if they get a very accurate impression of the countries they visit on these trips—they have such a short time in each place and are constantly wined and dined. Everywhere a great fuss is made over them. It's a marvelous opportunity and I certainly can't blame them for taking advantage of the opportunity and making the most of it. . . .

The pouch is in and no letters for me. Hope you're all well and that you're happy about Pat.

All my love,
Margy

✈ Ankara, Turkey
15 October 1945
Dearest Mother—
The mail finally came in. Have written one letter to you today, but the mail brought your letter of the 1st. You mustn't feel badly about Pat. Honestly, I really think it's good and I'm not worried about her at all. I know I'm not you. But darn, the struggles in a job. I love my work now and it's easy for me—the General told me the other day that I do the work of two WAC secretaries that he had before. Of course, they may have been pretty awful. And when I think back about all the jobs and all the years of work and I really have nothing to show for it—it's only now that I can make much more money than a living and I'm really enjoying living now—but even this can't go on indefinitely. I won't even feel badly if Pat and Du should have a child before Pat is 20. Suppose you think that's awful, but I don't. You know worry is fear and Pat and Du are not afraid. Fear is much worse than even the thing feared. Pat and Du are happy and brave and together they are very strong. And as Pat said the only thing that can spoil her happiness is that you are not as happy about it as she. So let her go with your blessing and be sincerely happy about her. Throw off your worries because they make you suffer so much and because there is no reason for worrying. I could give you dozens of reasons why it's good that she did this. Felt differently before because there were two sides and a choice of decisions—but since Pat felt so strongly about it there can be no doubt that it was the right thing to do. I think it's wonderful really I do. . . . I think it is wonderful that Du is so swell and that you all like

him so much. Not that Pat would have fallen in love with anyone but a swell person, but it would have been awful if you hadn't thought he was quite so swell. . . .

It's hard to write lots of times because I wonder if it doesn't sound like a bunch of malarkey to you half the time and I don't have time it seems to really settle down to think of all of you and your problems and write to you. I'm selfish and I write only about my interests here. I do think of you all often but I don't really "think" either. . . .

No more time now.
All my love,
Marge

✈ Ankara, Turkey
24 October 1945
Dear Mother—

Sunday the census was taken here. We had some people in the night before for chili and they didn't leave till three o'clock. At six in the morning guns were fired and no one was permitted to leave their house till the guns were fired the second time—expected to be about noon (actually was three in the morning)—and during that time the census takers were the only persons on the streets. Ours called on us at 7:00 A.M., but our maid Sultana took care of him and only awakened us to ask our ages. And we had been practicing for days how to answer all the questions.

The Fall is the most beautiful time of the year here. From September till Christmas the weather is marvelous. Balo and I went for a walk—after the census taking Sunday—and kicked through the leaves. . . .

Balo brought us a new lamp the other day—had it made out of an old peasant jug that has awfully nice lines and put a very nice parchment shade on it that he has had for some time. Everyone tells us how attractive our house is now and of course we know Balo deserves all the credit. It's full of things from him—vases, pictures, flowers, etc., etc. Besides I have countless personal gifts from him—bracelets, ear rings, silver cups and doo dads. And I'll never part with any of his gifts. . . .

Balo has his visa and is just waiting for transportation. May even leave the end of this week. When he gets to New York he will telephone you—so you will have a chance to thank him for being so nice to me. Of course, I'm going to miss him terribly but I'll see him in May or June whenever it is that I come home. If he's in Europe by then I'll do everything possible to see him on my way home. . . .

All my love,
Marge

✈ Ankara, Turkey
25 October 1945
Dear Pat and Du—

Have just this minute received your letter to Mother dated the 7th and telling about your wedding. The pouch is closing in a second so I can't really write a letter. . . .

It sounds wonderful, Pat, and you are so happy. Honestly I envy you very much.

Damn! I'm sitting here in the office with tears running down my face and I'm sure everyone thinks I'm a complete fool and they don't know what it's all about and I don't care. I feel so full I can't tell you about it but really it's marvelous and I know for certain that neither of you will ever regret it—words don't say the things I want to say—but I'm so happy for you and I love you both and I'll write very soon and what do you want for a wedding present? Wouldn't it be better if I sent you the money to buy it yourself? There is absolutely nothing here that you wouldn't pay three times the price—and even then nothing is so nice as the things you can buy in the States. I think Du will bear me out in that because I'm pretty sure it is the same in the Pacific—wherever the Americans have been and many places they haven't been, prices are fantastic.

My Balo is leaving on Monday by boat for the States and I'm going to miss him very much.

Very best love to you both,
[Marge]

✈ Ankara, Turkey
5 November 1945
Dearest Mother—

Just a note to tell you that four packages just arrived—haven't had time to open them yet but suppose they are four of the eight you said Lillian had sent. . . .

Balo left by boat for the States yesterday. He left Ankara a week before. Miss him very much of course. He will probably call you on the telephone soon after this letter arrives. The boat he is on expects to take 20 or 21 days for the trip so he should arrive just after Thanksgiving on the 25th or so.

I'm well and happy enough—will send you a long letter next pouch—cross my heart and promise. The weather is perfectly marvelous here.

All my love,
Marge

✈ Ankara, Turkey
21 November 1945
Dear Mother—

It's Thanksgiving Eve and I've been making arrangements for the General's Thanksgiving dinner party tomorrow night. Did all the invitations, have made the place cards and had to see the First Secretary [Earl L. Packer] at the Embassy—about the seating. That is a terrific problem because it must all be done according to protocol (or in the order their names appear on the diplomatic list). At the same time can't have husbands sitting next to or even very near their wives and there's always the problem of seating people together who have a language in common but that is not so important as protocol—and it may have to be that the person on one's right speaks nothing but Turkish and the one on your left speaks nothing but French. After the seating was settled Mrs. Packer, Ewart, and I went to Serge's (where the dinner is to be) to taste their version of a pumpkin pie. It really wasn't too bad except that they had baked the crust first and filled it with cooked (not baked) pumpkin pulp mixed with a couple of eggs and no spices that I could tell. Anyway, we explained how it should be as well as we could, and to try to be certain Mrs. Packer is going down tomorrow to taste it before they bake it, but still anything can happen. . . .

I miss Balo so much—all his thoughtfulness and endearing ways—and as you guessed, it was awful to be left here. I do hope things will go well for Balo in America. Ewart, Corelli, and Barbara are all very confident that they will. Balo is really a very, very swell person. . . .

Several girls have left here from the Embassy. Some completed their contracts and some resign and pay their own way back. Two of our favorites left last week—intending to take their time along the way—Athens, Rome, Paris, and Christmas in England. I'm afraid I'll never be impressed by people because they have seen foreign countries again—because it's so easy. . . .

I know that if Balo is ever near enough to S. Dak. he will certainly visit you. I should prefer to be there when he does though.

Getting too sleepy to write much more.

Thanksgiving Day 1945
Happy Thanksgiving!
Beautiful day here. Just came to the office for a minute and have been offered a ride home so must be on my way but wanted to get this in today's pouch.
All my love,
Marjorie

✈ Ankara, Turkey
5 December 1945
[Dear Lillian—]
. . . After Ewart and a few others leave, I'll be counting the days till I can get away. At least part of the time I am home, I'll probably spend it looking up people I've known here to talk over Ankara life. It's a very special sort of a place. We are always hearing of people who have left it being homesick for Ankara after they've gotten away—and some who were only casual acquaintances here, meeting by chance some other place, falling upon each other like long lost and dearest friends—then spending hours talking about people here. It's not true of all, but it's true of me and I know I'll be homesick for it, and I'm one of the very, very few who has been perfectly aware of it every moment I've been here. So many realize it only later. . . .

Awfully anxious to hear from Balo—and of course that reunion will really be something. I hope it won't be disappointing for either of us, but it may be. But it just can't be. We will have a million, million things to talk about.

I'm still talking about my world and now I'm sleepy. Another thing about my world—thoroughly enjoy my work. Have never had a job I like better and I'm sort of confident that I won't have any trouble getting another assignment. . . .

Good night and best love to all,

Marge

✈ Ankara, Turkey

26 November 1945

Dear Dad and Mother:

. . . Received a letter from Balo a couple day ago—written on the boat and mailed at Algiers. He is supposed to arrive in New York today. . . .

Our Thanksgiving party was fine. I'll tell you about it in the next pouch. . . .

Went out with a Major from Iowa the other night. He's nice and rather fun in a group but dull alone. It was nice of Karl Mundt to write you [see Appendix 3]. A good politician I would say. Those who talked with him here liked him—nice to have a South Dakotan make a good impression. Not that I'm not proud of S.D. because I am—but so many have never known anyone from there and they have to be convinced.

All my love,

Marge

✈ Ankara, Turkey

16 December 1945

Dear Mother—

. . . Have had two letters from Balo from New York. They were both written within the first three days he was there. He said he thought we would like his American haircut. He advised me to come home by plane or a comfortable liner but never by a liberty ship. A few days later he went to Washington—I received a cable signed "Sally [Norbeck and] Balo" so I know they got together and I was awfully thrilled— but haven't had a letter from either since they met. . . .

Ted is coming to Ankara Saturday or Sunday morning so will have lots of dancing. Christmas Eve we're going to the Embassy for buffet supper. . . .

Afraid Ewart and Ted will be going home in a few months. . . . Glad I have only a few months to go—the place is getting too full of memories for me—like a ghost town. Marian left last week and I wept again. . . .

Barbara will be leaving Ankara soon after Christmas. She's going to Istanbul for a couple of months to work—then home. Georgia [M. Martinov]—the Ambassador's secretary—is moving in with us then. Wish we could afford to keep it for just Corelli and me but we want to save as much as possible and it will be cheaper with three of course. . . .

Must write to Balo—

Love to all of you,

Marjorie

✈ Ankara, Turkey

17 December 1945

Dear Dad and Mother—

Had such a good day's mail—letters from Balo (after he'd met Sally), Sally (before she met Balo), two letters from Mother and one of them included a note from Lillian, a card from Ellen (the girl I came to Turkey with), a letter from Pat, and another enclosed from Pat with one of your letters. . . . How I feel like writing to everyone. . . .

Don't understand Balo's not calling you. He hasn't mentioned it so I'm pretty sure he hasn't tried. I still think he will call you. . . .

Loved Pat's letter. She is so happy and she very generously wished she could give me some because it seemed more than her share. Then as a postscript she said I didn't have to tell her but, she said, "You are in love with Balo aren't you." That was nice.

I don't know about coming home. It will be this summer certainly but by boat or plane—thru the Pacific or Europe I don't know. It will probably be either direct from Istanbul by boat thru the Mediterranean to New York or thru Europe—Athens—Rome—Paris—London by air then by boat from England. Some of the State Dept. girls have gone that way—or by boat from France—Corelli will have to stay till September or October. . . .

Must write to others—
Best love,
Marjorie

✈ Ankara, Turkey
3 January 1946
Dearest Lillian—

. . . Christmas and New Years were both lots of fun. Ted came Sunday morning before Christmas and left on Thursday night. We were busy every minute—lunch every day and dinner and dancing every night and cocktail parties and people dropping in all the time. I was exhausted when it was over. Ted wanted me to come to Istanbul for New Years but I said "No." Not that I was enthused at the prospect of New Years Eve plans here but as it turned out that was fun too.

Can't give you details on all the parties but New Years Eve was probably the most interesting. Admiral W. L. Jackson, the British Navel Attaché (called A. J.) had a small [cocktail] party. . . . Then down to the [Ankara Palas] dining room and there were several hundred Turks in evening clothes. . . . Except for three or four other people, we were the only non-Turks present. Had a marvelous dinner—lobster, wines and stuff. We all got noisemakers and threw streamers and danced. Once when we got sort of scattered, someone rounded us up and said A. J. wanted us back to the table. When we got back, found the Prime Minister on his way and he sat with us for about a half an hour. Have never sat at the same table with him before but we have a nodding and smiling acquaintance at Karpiç where he has lunch every day. He doesn't speak English—only French and Turkish and probably German. But the conversation was in French at the table. Once he asked me if I could say "I love you" in Turkish—gave me quite a turn because I hadn't been paying any attention to what he was saying and suddenly the Prime Minister was looking directly at me and saying in English, "I love you"—with prompt from the side I managed to say it in Turkish. . . . We left the Ankara Palas sometime after midnight and went down to Serge's to finish the night. Intended to out stay everyone but got too sleepy and I was in bed by seven—and slept through till six that night. . . .

I am awfully disappointed about the mail, wanted to hear more from Balo too. Had a cable from him yesterday but it was just "All love." Wish he were still here but of course he has to get on with the business of living—rather making a new life for himself and possibly for us.

Best love to all of you,

Marjorie

✈ Ankara, Turkey

23 January 1946

Dearest Mom—

Just got your letter [about surgery, probably for colon cancer] of the 7th and Lillian's of the 8th. Knowing that the cables aren't being delivered, I'm sick. We think there may be more mail tomorrow so I'm hoping for more news. Gosh I'm still weak. I think my heart stopped beating and I held my breath all the time I read the letter.[37]

All my love, Marjorie

[P.S.] All my very best wishes for a very quick recovery—I'm sure it will be a relief to you to have it over. Take care of yourself now—I'm going to send you another check next week—this time you must spend it for pleasure—not an operation. For a real celebration—not an ether jag. . . .

✈ Ankara, Turkey

28 January 1946

Dear Mother—

I sent a cable to Balo on Friday [25 January 1946] to telephone Lillian and cable a reply to me. I don't know how long it will take for him to get it although they say cables are delivered to New York, S.F. [San Francisco], and Washington. They were very nice at the Embassy, offered to cable the Department in Washington (signed by the Ambassador), have them contact you and cable back. The mail is so bad that writing a daily letter doesn't help me much. You see last week I got the one you wrote on the 7th and the one Lillian wrote on the 8th, and although some may come in today, mail is not expected till Thursday. . . .

Twenty days since you had the operation. Hope you are well over it now and relieved to have it over.

All my love,
Marjorie

⤷ Ankara, Turkey
7:30 A.M.
29 January 1946
Mother darling,
Woke up so early this morning and feeling so depressed. Now I'm worrying about you. There may be a cable from Balo today. . . .

Hope I hear very soon that you are feeling wonderful—and that everyone else in the family is too. Lillian has been so good. I know it has been very difficult for her to go through all of this.

Love to all and to you especially,
Marjorie

⤷ Ankara, Turkey
4 February 1946
Dear Mother—
. . . I sent in my resignation—actually only a request for transportation—for May. The General has asked me to change my mind, said he wants me to stay as long as I will. Told him I still might extend it about three months but would talk with him when we had more time. The result of the talk will be a promotion and I may stay a little longer. . . .

It was awful to hear about your having the operation. . . . I sent the cable to Balo on Friday. He must have received it and called you on Saturday because his cable was dated Saturday and I didn't receive it until Tuesday. Had left word with the maid to call the office as soon as a cable arrived. She got only the notice as she was out when it did come and that was the day I was up writing a letter to you at 7:30 a.m. Ewart had the chauffeur waiting at the door for me before he told me there was a cable at the post office and we drove like mad. Until that day I had felt certain everything was all right with you—and even that day I was not prepared if it hadn't been all right. I was terribly relieved anyway of course. . . . I'm awfully glad I cabled. It was fortunate that Balo was in New York. Although either the Ambassador or the General would have done it officially—but "officially" would have taken longer. . . .

Like my job and like my friends, but must come home this year to be re-Americanized. Then out again. . . .

Take care of yourselves—all of you—

Best love,

Marjorie

⇥ Ankara, Turkey

10 February 1946

Dearest Lillian—

. . . I do want to see all of you very much and I think it's necessary to come home to be re-Americanized, but I like foreign service so much that if it were not for Balo—I'm sure I'd stay over another year. Then I would get home leave with transportation home and not have to re-sign to get it. Next time I go out I may do that, but I really think two years is enough for the first stretch.

It's been a month since Mother's operation. That letter you wrote announcing it really shattered me. . . . I've been lucky (touch wood) in not picking up the usual—dysentery, malaria, tape worm & such—they are all terrible and all common. Often strikes people after they get back to the States so I won't boast till I've been home. . . .

Love to all of you,

Marge

⇥ Ankara, Turkey

13 February 1946

Dear Mother—

. . . Corelli and I wondered what Lillian's reaction to Balo's tele-phone call was. He doesn't have a good voice on the telephone—in fact it's pretty awful and doesn't sound like him. Anyway that with his accent may have given her an odd impression. He's such a swell person though. I'm very anxious to see him again. . . .

Had an awfully nice letter from Pat. She's certainly a happy girl.

Love to all of you,

Marge

✈ Ankara, Turkey

22 February 1946

Dear Mother—

. . . I have decided definitely to leave in May and I am literally counting the days. Don't send any more things but don't worry about anything you may have sent—or if you've already bought things for me,
get them off immediately and then don't shop any more. If they should
arrive after I leave, Corelli will take care of them. . . .

Monday nights are special for Balo and me so I never go out with
anyone tete a tete on Mondays but in a group it's all right. . . .

I may not know until just before I leave what route I will take home.
If Washington insists that I must return by boat from here, that's what
I will have to do—but if they say "by any means" I'll probably go by air
to Athens, Rome, Paris, and London and by boat from England. Or
possibly by train from Rome to Paris. I'm afraid that I may be so restless to get home that I won't mind going by boat from Istanbul direct
to New York and just thumb my nose at Europe. You know there's not
a doubt in my mind that I won't leave the U.S. again—much as I love
"my own, my native land." Corny but you don't appreciate it till you
get away. . . .

Best love,

[Marge]

✈ Ankara, Turkey

5 March 1946

Dearest Sally [with carbon copy to Mother]—

. . . Have gotten sort of tired of the parties here and am staying away
from them. There are so many and even at this moment I should be
drinking champagne at a reception—but there will be so many people,
no one will notice my absence. You know a decoration of crossed cocktail glasses has been suggested for people who have served a tour of
duty in Ankara. Another suggestion is a kidney pierced with a screwdriver—that being the famous cocktail here (half orange juice and half
votka). I mean "screwdriver" is the name of that cocktail.

Now I have a new and very absorbing interest that will make these
last ten weeks pass more quickly. Admiral Jackson, the British Naval

Attaché, is having his portrait done in oil by a Turkish artist—Tuna Saip.[38] One day last week I visited Saip's studio with A. J. Saip asked if he might do a crayon sketch of me so I went back on Sunday and sat for him for three hours. It was lots of fun. He did the head and shoulders, life-size. Everyone thinks I look too stern in it, but they all agree that the eyes and forehead are excellent and that anyone would recognize me. . . . The other day he let me rest about every 20 minutes and invited criticism which I gave. It was interesting to watch the thing change. A. J. has been there about 20 times and of course knows all the paintings perfectly. We had a very enthusiastic discussion about them, and I brought out a couple of Polish nudes, prints that Balo had given Corelli. We compared the style of them with Saip's. As I was putting them away I realized that our lively conversation was completely unembarrassed, and it reminded me of that first visit to the Corcoran Art Gallery with you when I confessed to you that it embarrassed me to look at those nude statues—and you of course were amused and embarrassed me even more by telling everyone about it. It seems that that girl from the country is getting some sophistication possibly.

[Marge]

✈ Ankara, Turkey
6 March 1946
Dear Mother—
. . . I'm enclosing the picture of the New Year's party that I said I would send. Shall probably send you a photograph of the sketch referred to in the letter to Sally. Wrote much more to Sally but the rest was just for Sally and you wouldn't be interested. Tomorrow Saip (pronounced Sah-heep) starts the oil. Ted has written from Istanbul that I will probably get over the last traces of embarrassment and acquire complete sophistication if I will pose as Saip would probably prefer. If I will, he says he can look forward to seeing me hanging in some gallery in Istanbul in the "altogether."

Gosh I'm getting so anxious to be on my homeward way I'm practically a fliberty giberty—whatever that is, but it sounds like me. Corelli is asking for permission to leave in July—two months before her contract will be finished and wanted me to promise the General I would stay till then if he would approve—believing that might have some influence with him. I don't know about that but after 24 hours of thinking about it, I found it impossible to change my plans and agree to say on the extra time. Of course I would be paid for it. I could probably stay here and be paid for it the rest of my life if I wanted to, and not even "probably" because I could. Anyway May it will be but don't expect me in S.D. till probably the middle of June.

Much love to all of you,
Margie

✈ Ankara, Turkey
22 March 1946
Dear Mother—

. . . Washington has authorized my travel by any means so unless things change a whole lot, I'll return via Cairo, Athens, Rome, Paris and London. . . . Two State Department girls left the first week in November. They had a marvelous trip and spent three months—one did and the other nearly four. I won't take that long but don't expect me till I get there. They've ordered me to Washington for 30 days temporary duty on per diem—then they intend to reassign me of course. Although I'll have to report to Washington, expect I'll take leave before I start the 30 days.

Everyone is excited about the USS *Missouri* arriving in Istanbul the first week in April.[39] Our friend, Cadri Rizan, Chief of Protocol, for whom we gave a cocktail party, is returning on it, escorting the body of the Turkish Ambassador to the U.S. who died last year. Corelli and I think one day that we will go down for it—because there will be lots of parties and lots of Americans—and the next day we think we won't. Georgia is going with the Ambassador and a suite has been reserved for Corelli, Georgia, and me at the hotel. I want one more trip to Istanbul before I leave, but also I'm being extremely careful with my money; yet it will be very exciting to see the *Missouri* come in. . . .

Love to all of you,
Marjorie

→ Ankara. Turkey
29 March 1946
Dear Mother—

... Wonder how long it will take to get home. They say that at the moment there is such a backlog in Paris and even worse in England that one may be held up weeks at either place.[40] Gosh I wouldn't mind being held in France in May or June—but I'd like to be there with Balo. He's getting awfully anxious for me to come home and maybe I'll be able to help him a little. Because my orders will read to Washington for 30 days' temporary duty and new orders, I'll get a higher priority than if I were resigning or going home on furlough orders.[41] May even whisk through in record time, especially if the backlogs are cleared by that time—but I hope I'll have at least a few days at some of the places. ...

Love to all,
Margie

→ Istanbul, Turkey
Tuesday, 9 April 1946
Dearest [Balo]—

The *Missouri* has gone but now that I'm here I'm going to stay on a few more days. The weather is marvelous and I'm having a fine time but not much sleep. ... The Turks have been terribly impressed by the visit. They have issued special *Missouri* stamps, *Missouri* cigarettes and stuff. I'll tell you all about the visit when I get home. There have been lots of parties and it has been fun. ... Sunday Georgia, Corelli, and I went out to the ship for the first time. We went out in one of the fast little launches the ship carries. It was thrilling to see the thing and as we approached we noticed there was lots of excitement and men were standing along the rail signaling for us to continue down the side. We finally got the word that there was a man overboard and another little launch was scurrying around. Our launch called over to them, "Did you get him," and there was a young red-headed freckled kid standing up, feet apart, chest out and a broad grin—he just pointed to himself that it was he who had been in the water. They assured us that it doesn't happen often. The battleship was so solid, when we were on it there was no sensation of being on the water at all. Of course we stood on The Spot where the peace [with Japan] was signed. The officers and men were all very nice and seeing them so many times while they were here we got to know them. They were all so fine—made me awfully proud of Americans. . . .

I met and talked with Admirals and Commodores, ensigns, commanders and everyone. Sort of made friends with a couple of seamen too who played in the orchestra. They played at the Consulate's reception and at the Palace too and when I would go off to dance, I often left my drink or my bag or both at their feet. Once when the orchestra changed and a Turkish orchestra took over, this youngster came weaving through the crowd to me to give me my bag because he wouldn't be sitting there for awhile. They were all so nice and it made me homesick for America.

After the reception on the ship, the pilot asked me to stay on for the movies and I wanted to, but I had kept Ted and Georgia waiting because I'd been promised a 5-gallon keg of Coca Cola syrup and they were having trouble digging it out of the supply room. Anyway, the Americans in Ankara are going to be grateful to the *Missouri* for that Coca Cola. . . . I was supposed to go on for the dance [at the Pera Palas] at 10 o'clock, but neither Georgia nor I felt like going into long dress again (just realized it's finally happened—didn't think the day would ever come that I would think it too much trouble to get into a long dress).[42] Anyway when the car came for me I sent it away.

12 April 1946
Dear Mother—
The above is a copy of a letter to Balo. . . .
Have my reservation to Cairo on BOAC May 16th & I'm trying to get a reservation on TWA from Cairo to New York.[43] Don't think I'll dilly dally along the way & if I go right through it's only 2 days from Cairo to New York. Expect I'll see all of you the first part of June.
Much love,
Margie

⤙ Ankara, Turkey
16 April 1946
Dearest [Balo]—

Only four more Sundays in Turkey and, after today, 21 days (5-day week) at the office. It's very exciting to think about and I have much to do.

We saw Ewart and Bill [William F. Ross, assistant United States military attaché] off on the Taurus last night. Miss them very much after seeing them every day for such a long time—nearly all the time I've been in Turkey—at the office, our Club, and at parties. Had the usual Taurus farewell and even poured racki on Bill's hat and he got on the train with his hat on fire. We couldn't get confetti but threw rice on them. . . .

Jeff is leaving on BOAC Thursday. Talked with him a minute at Ewart's house last night and he too is looking forward to seeing you again. . . .

Everyone is leaving and the new ones coming out are not so interesting as the ones who have gone. Corelli this morning said that if she could leave in my place on May 16th and I would stay till July 15th (the date she expects to leave) she would pay me a thousand dollars. Do you think I should? I can't do it of course, even if it could be approved. After lunch.

We had Jean Brennan [of the Office of the Counselor for Economic Affairs] and Barbara at the house for lunch today. It was very pleasant. Our house is pleasant, and Corelli and I often speak of how much more attractive it is than when we first moved in—and everywhere I look there are reminders of you, things you have given us. Everyone who comes comments on how nice it is and they always come again. I enjoyed Istanbul and Istanbul is beautiful. The Bosporus is beautiful and I don't think any city could possibly have the wonderful skyline that Istanbul has. But I still prefer Ankara and was glad to come back.

We're going to have one of those American girls luncheons at Karpitch's on Saturday this week. Think it will be fun and sort of looking forward to it. Haven't had one for months and months. About five or six girls who came a month or two ago, I don't even know. They're different from the first lot and we don't see them around very much. The luncheon is to celebrate our new adjustment in allowances which amounts to an increase for all of us. Wish it had started earlier so I could benefit more from it. . . .

There are so many things to talk about. I'm wishing the days away till I can leave. It's awful to stay here and say goodbye to people. Yours was a selfish wish to be the first to leave but I had the same wish—only I didn't get mine. At least Corelli and Ted will have to stay and say goodbye to me. Ted's replacement has been named and he will leave as soon as the new colonel arrives—probably in June. I certainly hope so as he needs to go home. It will be three years this June since he left the States. Mrs. Ted is getting a little put out over the prolonged absence I think and Ted has wanted to go home for a long long time. By the way, remember your suggestion that they be our first weekend guests. I told Ted and he accepted for the whole family and with pleasure. . . .

I did get your cable on my birthday. I thought I wrote you about it. Corelli didn't get your letter about the flowers till long after my birthday, but Virginia sent me flowers on that day with a card which she signed for herself and also as "Balo's messenger." It was awfully sweet of her. Have missed the flowers you sent me so often. Corelli and Georgia gave a dinner party the day before my birthday and after midnight everyone wished me a happy birthday. . . . The last three years the birthdays have at least been unusual—my 31st was the best. . . . We'll celebrate our birthdays together next year perhaps.

When I started this letter I made a carbon copy for Mother but didn't expect to write so much gossip about people they don't know. It won't be of much interest to them but begging your forgiveness, shall send it to them anyway.

[Marge]

Ankara, Turkey
19 April 1946
Dear Mother—
Only 26 days and I'll be on my way. When you get this it will be much less. Haven't heard from Cairo yet, whether they were able to get a reservation on TWA for me. I'm enclosing a copy of a letter written to Balo. . . .

Just came from a champagne luncheon for Corelli's birthday and have eaten too much.

Am so excited about leaving. I don't know how long I'll stay nor what I'll do after. Have loved it here—it has been wonderful but of course I shall not come back to Turkey to work and only possibly to visit. But now I'm terribly thrilled to realize that I'll be home again so soon. "Home" is a pretty vague word for me though—has lots of meanings and in a way none at all. I don't think less of any of you of course but you understand, I'm sure, I've been away for so long—years before I came here. Things have changed so much for me. I wonder how much I've changed. Probably I'd better come home without Balo, rather than take a chance on you having two strangers on your hands. I know you all love Balo and Balo loves all of you—but you know each other only through my eyes. I've also written that to Balo (you didn't get a copy of the entire letter of course) but also told him that if he's free to get away and wants to (I know he wants to) then to plan on visiting Redfield with me—but we can decide that and other things when I get to New York. He's a love and I'm awfully anxious to see him too. He writes wonderful letters. Have had two in the past three days written April 6th and 9th. Life with him—oh well have time to decide. I know I'm crazy. More from thought of going home than from the champagne.

See you soon!
Much love to all of you,
Marjorie

→ Ankara, Turkey
24 April 1946
Dear Mother—
. . . Only three weeks from tomorrow I'll be leaving Ankara. Have been talking about it for so long and dreaming about it—it hardly seems possible that the time is so near. Transportation is extremely difficult to arrange—either by boat or air. I'll do whatever seems best about stopovers, but I hope it won't be my only opportunity. I don't think it will be. . . .

I'll miss Corelli and Georgia. It has been fun living with them. We laugh a lot. . . .

It's been a very happy time for me and certainly the most profitable two years of my life. "Profitable" personally mostly—financially it could have been better if I had taken advantage, but wouldn't I have lost something personally? I think—as it is—it's been better financially than it would have been if I had stayed at home. It's hard to tell what I value most in the experience—whether it's the good fortune of having friends—good friends. Impossible to develop that—take too long—but there are lots of things I value. One of the many that I shall never again be awed by people who have "traveled." Now that I've done it, I know that anyone can & no one should be impressed at all when someone speaks of foreign places familiarly.

Must go to bed—See you all very soon.

Much love,

Marjorie

⟩⟨ Cumberland Hotel
Marble Arch
London, England
25 May 1946
Dearest Family—

Have been on the way since the 16th. Cabled Balo yesterday because it was only then that I knew definitely that I would leave from England and the date. I'm sailing on a transport called the *Holbrook* and expecting it may be pretty awful if the stories about these brides and babies are true. The transports are all full of them.[44] I should arrive during the first week of June and of course will telephone you from New York. Sailing date is the 28th, Tuesday, but I leave London for Southampton early Monday morning.

England is supposed to be at its best now and it is lovely. I came from Cairo on a British plane—we landed . . . near Bournemouth and came by train to London from there.

I've been running around like mad since I got here getting the transportation fixed up. . . .

Have some acquaintances here and people are awfully nice but I wish Balo were with me. Anyway a few days in a place isn't enough. One should have weeks and an energetic, enthusiastic, and congenial companion. Balo and I are going to do France together, and Italy, Greece, and the Balkans, and sometime the Orient. I have great dreams, but after getting away once it doesn't seem impossible at all.

There's much to write about but I'm sort of rushed at the moment and I'll see you soon anyway. Hope you're all well. It was hard to leave Turkey. Guess I still have lots of friends there—there were parties, luncheons, cocktails, and dinners every day the last week & I saw the sun rise several times. Lots of people were at the airport.... After they said it was time to get on the plane, it took another ten minutes to kiss everyone goodbye and Corelli cried, bless her heart. I didn't—I felt sort of sick. I had never seen Corelli cry before....

The two years were pretty wonderful and thank goodness I realized it while I was there. So many don't appreciate it till they leave—rather after they've left. That's over now and I hope Ted was right when he said there are other Ankaras ahead for me....

It's marvelous to sleep in good beds again.... The first night I was here I slept like one unconscious. I had been on the plane all the night before and the landings were very bad. After each takeoff I couldn't sleep for thinking of the next landing. The men on the plane admitted afterward that they were as frightened as I. I have never known such clumsy landings, and I think it was only the grace of God that let us walk away from the first two.

The nights at Cairo were horrible and I was sick there and I'm the worst kind of baby when I'm sick. It was the intense heat, filth, and flies. I got gyppy and felt faint during the day. The evenings were cooler so felt better but didn't sleep well. It's true what they say about Shepheard's terrace—if you sit there long enough you'll see the whole world pass by. The first evening there, saw at least ten people I knew.

Must go now. See you soon.

Love,

Marge

NOTES

1. See the Introduction, pp. 11–12, for information on the role and responsibilities of military attachés during World War II.

2. Wendell L. Willkie, *One World* (New York: Simon & Schuster, 1943), pp. 37–49. Willkie was the unsuccessful Republican nominee for president in 1940. During 1941 and 1942, he traveled throughout the world as President Franklin D. Roosevelt's personal representative. Chapter 3 of *One World* is based on his travels in Turkey.

3. Mrs. McLarren was a Washington fortuneteller, whose daughter Mabel worked for the State Department in Ankara.

4. The articles Havreberg referenced were Maynard Owen Williams, "Turkey, Where Earthquakes Followed Timur's Trail," *National Geographic* 77 (Mar. 1940): 395–406, and Edward Stevenson Murray, "On the Turks' Russian Frontier," *National Geographic* 80 (Sept. 1941): 367–92.

5. After Havreberg gave up her apartment, she lived, rent free, with her friend, Dorothy.

6. Lemons are a home remedy for motion sickness. The acid in lemons reduces saliva and eases the nausea associated with motion sickness.

7. A dragoman functions as interpreter, translator, and official guide in Turkish-, Arabic-, and Persian-speaking countries.

8. On the significance of Karpiç's and its legendary owner Baba Karpiç in wartime Ankara, see the Introduction, pp. 10–12, and Appendix No. 1, "Karptich the Magnificent." The 13 May 1944 *Saturday Evening Post* article to which Havreberg refers is "Baba Walks a Tightrope," by George Moorad, p. 6.

9. Earl L. Packer was First Secretary at the United States Embassy in Ankara. Republique Turque, Ministère des Affaires Etrangères, *Liste du Corps Diplomatique* (Ankara, Turkey: n.p., 1945), p. 15, copy in the Marjorie Havreberg Steinbach Jenkins Papers, State Archives Collection, South Dakota State Historical Society, Pierre.

10. The Shepheard Hotel in Cairo traces its origins to 1841 when Samuel Shepheard from Northumberland, England, became the manger of the British Hotel in Cairo. Four years later, he bought the British Hotel and changed its name to Shepheard. Until it burned in 1952, the Shepheard Hotel welcomed kings, queens, heads of states, and international personalities. During World War II, Shepheard's served as a rendezvous for prominent Allied officers, politicians, and spies. The modern-day Shepheard Hotel is located near the site of the original hotel.

11. *See* Appendix No. 2 for a copy of Karpiç's luncheon menu for 16 August 1944.

12. The muezzin summons Muslims to prayer five times a day.

13. For censorship of letters during World War II, *See* D'Ann Campbell, *Women at War with America: Private Lives in a Patriotic Era* (Cambridge, Mass.: Harvard University Press, 1984), pp. 71–72, 200.

14. The Taurus Express was a luxury passenger train that connected Cairo to Istanbul (via Ankara). At Istanbul, passengers of the Taurus Express could transfer to its sister luxury service, the Simplon Orient Express, both of which were run by the Compagnie Internationale des Wagon-Lits. The routes of the two express trains, which jointly ran from London to Baghdad, were featured in Agatha Christie's famous mystery *Murder on the Orient Express* (1934).

15. Following the liberation of Paris on 25 August 1944, representatives of the Vichy French, the government that had collaborated with the Axis powers, were forced to vacate the embassy in Ankara. For the liberation of Paris, *see* John Keegan, *The Second World War* (New York: Penguin Group, 1990), pp. 410–14.

16. The Chinese ringneck pheasant is the state bird of South Dakota, where pheasant hunting is a fall ritual. During the war, ammunition could be hard to acquire, but during the depression, pheasants had been a staple on many family tables. *See* James Marten, "'We Always Looked Forward to the Hunters Coming': The Culture of Pheasant Hunting in South Dakota," *South Dakota History* 29 (Summer 1999): 87–112 and Helen J. Bergh, "Troop Trains and Pheasant Sandwiches: The Aberdeen Canteen in World War II," *South Dakota History* 23 (Summer 1993): 133–41.

17. Because Ambassador Steinhardt's wife suffered from various medical problems, the couple's daughter often took her mother's place at formal events. Igor Lukes, "Ambassador Laurence Steinhardt: From New York to Prague," *Diplomacy and Statecraft* 17 (2006): 525, 535.

18. The Polish resistance led the sixty-three-day Warsaw Uprising to liberate the city from Nazi occupation. It began on 1 August and ended in tragic failure on 2 October 1944. The casualty count was enormous. For more on the uprising, *see* Aleksander Gieysztor, "The Warsaw Uprising in the Europe of 1944," *Dialogue and Universalism* 14 (June 2004): 13–22.

19. On 7 November 1944, Democratic president Franklin D. Roosevelt was elected for an unprecedented fourth term, defeating Republican governor Thomas E. Dewey of New York. Ted Morgan, *FDR: A Biography* (New York: Simon & Schuster, 1985), pp. 737–40. Because of the seven-hour time difference between the East Coast of the United States and Turkey, it would be later on the morning of 8 November before the election results would be known in Ankara.

20. Many artists recorded the song "Margie" (1920) and by the 1940s, it had become a jazz standard. The United Service Organizations (USO) was formed early in 1941, bringing together six social-service organizations that had provided assistance to United States troops during World War I. During World War II, the USO sponsored dances, entertainment, and other types of recreational activities for uniformed personnel both at home and abroad. Famous entertainers, such as Bob Hope, Judy

Garland, and Bing Crosby, performed in USO shows for American troops stationed around the world.

21. Following the Nazi invasion of Yugoslavia in April 1941, Yugoslavian king Peter II established a royal government-in-exile in London. Milo Talbot was the nineteen-year-old son of the Yugoslavian ambassador representing the royal government-in-exile.

22. The Czechoslovakian government-in-exile in England had appointed Dr. Milos Hanak to be its ambassador to Turkey. *Liste du Corps Diplomatique*, p. 61.

23. Prior to formation of the state of Israel in 1948, Palestine was the name used to describe the area between the Mediterranean Sea and the Jordan River and various adjoining lands.

24. Early in 1945, Ambassador Steinhardt learned that he would become ambassador to Czechoslovakia. He left Turkey on 1 April 1945. Lukes, "Ambassador Laurence Steinhardt," p. 539.

25. Jack, born in 1936, and Sally, born in 1939, were the children of Havreberg's sister Lillian and her husband Duke Enstrom.

26. Şükrü Saracoğlu was Prime Minister of Turkey from 1942 to 1946. A special table at Karpiç's was always reserved for the prime minister. Moorad, "Baba Walks a Tightrope," p. 6.

27. President Franklin D. Roosevelt died on 12 April 1945. His death ushered in a month of mourning at all United States government offices.

28. Havreberg and Paul Steinbach were divorced in May 1945, but Marjorie makes no direct reference to the event in her letters. Havreberg's lawyers filed the divorce degree on 1 May 1945 in Pierre, South Dakota. Steinbach was not present and did not contest the divorce.

29. Maynard Owen Williams, "The Turkish Republic Comes of Age," *National Geographic* 87 (May 1945): 581–600.

30. At the end of World War II, a Soviet-controlled Polish government was established in Warsaw. Since Colonel Zimnal represented the anti-communist Polish government-in-exile headquartered in London, it would not have been appropriate for Poles and Russians to be seated at the same table.

31. This occasion actually marked the third time that it was daylight when Havreberg went to bed. She evidently forgot about her celebrations bringing in the 1945 New Year. *See* her letter of 4 Jan. 1945.

32. Blood on the toothbrush is a symptom of periodontal disease. Untreated periodontal disease can lead to tooth loss.

33. The United States dropped atomic bombs on Hiroshima and Nagasaki, Japan, on 6 and 9 August 1945. The *Buck Rogers in the 25th Century* comic strip made its first appearance on 7 January 1929. The adventures of Buck Rogers, often called "space opera," have also been featured in movies as well as radio and television shows. Keegan, *Second World War*, p. 584.

34. The initial announcement of Japan's surrender came on the afternoon of 14 August 1945. Because of time zone differences, it was 15 August in the United States and Europe. The formal surrender occurred aboard the USS *Missouri* docked in Tokyo Bay on 2 September 1945.

35. Previous letters contained considerable discussion about whether Havreberg's eighteen-year-old sister Patricia should marry George ("Du") DuChateau, a young enlisted man in the navy. Havreberg had urged her sister, who had graduated from high school in June 1945, to postpone marriage and continue her education, but the marriage of Patricia and Du in the fall of 1945 was not totally unexpected.

36. Karl E. Mundt was a Republican representing South Dakota in the United States House of Representatives from 1938 to 1948 and in the Senate from 1948 to 1973. *See* Appendix No. 3 for a copy of the 22 October 1945 letter Mundt wrote to Havreberg's parents about his visit to Ankara and their daughter. Mundt visited Ankara as a member of the House Foreign Affairs Committee, along with Congresswoman Frances P. Bolton, Republican from Ohio, who served in the House from 1940 to 1969. During World War II, she was a strong proponent of women in the military. Herbert S. Schell, *History of South Dakota*, 4th ed., rev. John E. Miller (Pierre: South Dakota State Historical Society Press, 2004), p. 344.

37. Bessie Havreberg would die of colon cancer in December 1947.

38. Saip Tuna (1904–1974) studied art in Turkey, Germany, and France. He was known for his fine portraits of Ataturk and compositions featuring that leader. He sketched a portrait of Ataturk at Karpiç's restaurant and also did charcoal pencil drawing of his friends. "Saip Tuna," *Turkish Paintings*, www.turkishpaintings.com. Tuna's sketch of Havreberg is included in the illustrations.

39. The battleship that served as the site for the formal surrender of Japan on 2 September 1945, the USS *Missouri*, rode at anchor in the Bosporus from 5 to 9 April 1946 to deliver the remains of the body of Munir Ertegun, the Turkish ambassador to the United States who had died in Washington in November 1944.

40. The redeployment to the United States of millions of American troops stationed in Europe at the end of the war did not go smoothly, and backlogs continued until well into 1946. The military developed a point system of demobilization based on service longevity, overseas duty, combat, and parenthood, but personnel stationed abroad continually complained about the system and delays.

41. For a copy of Havreberg's orders to Washington, D.C., *see* Appendix No. 4, Special Order No. 28, 18 April 1946.

42. The Pera Palace Hotel, which opened in 1892, was originally built for passengers on the Orient Express. Many famous people have stayed there, including Atatürk, Ismet Inönü, Alfred Hitchcock, Greta Garbo, and Agatha Christie.

43. British Overseas Airways Corporation (BOAC) was the British state airline from 1939 to 1974, when it merged with British European Airways Corporation to

become British Airways. Trans World Airlines (TWA) was a major United States airline from 1930 until 2001, when it was acquired by American Airlines.

44. The *Holbrook* was one of several ships that transported some seventy thousand British war brides and their babies to America to be reunited with their GI husbands and fathers. Havreberg is referring to widespread newspaper coverage about nine babies who had died from a mysterious illness during an April 1946 voyage on the *Holbrook*.

Epilogue

With Havreberg's return to the United States in early June 1946, she and Balinski were reunited. They then traveled to Redfield to visit Havreberg's family. Photographs from this visit depict a joyous and loving gathering. After the summer of 1946, however, Balinski faded from the picture. Other than a brief postcard from Balinski from San Francisco on 5 January 1948 and occasional references to Balinski in letters that Ankara friends wrote to Havreberg, little information about his post-World-War-II life appears in her papers. It is only with Balinski's death on 6 January 1990 that he re-emerges. Balinski's son, Michel Balinski, then living in Paris with his wife and children, sent a death announcement to Havreberg at her home near Detroit Lakes, Minnesota, where she then lived. At the time of his death, Balinski lived in Quito, Ecuador, where he had served as representative to the United Nations Technical Commission. Like many representatives of the Polish government-in-exile, he had not returned to Communist-controlled Poland.

Balinski's death prompted Havreberg to write a long letter to Jeffrey Short, a colleague and friend with whom she and Balinski had shared many adventures in Ankara. She fondly recalled their good times together in Turkey and wrote that Balo's death "has made me very sad." She continued: "It has been more than forty years since the last time I saw him—and it doesn't make sense but I'll miss him. He did write to me in 1986, I replied, and the following Christmas he sent a Christmas greeting. I didn't write again. I wish I had." She reiterated that Ankara represented "a very happy time" in her life and that the news about Balinski had made her nostalgic. She concluded, "It doesn't get easier to lose someone I care about."[1] After more than four decades, Balinski still held a special place in Havreberg's heart.

But Havreberg's life took a different path. Following her visit to her family in June 1946, she took a six-month leave of absence from her work. In late January 1947, she returned to Washington, D.C., and in August 1947, she was assigned to a clerical position with the Office of the Military Attaché in Ottawa, Canada. However, she resigned this position in October and returned to Redfield to help care for her mother, who was suffering from colon cancer. In December, Bessie Havreberg died.

During this difficult period, Havreberg reconnected with Tom Jenkins, who continued to work at Minot State Teacher's College in North Dakota. His letters to Havreberg help shed light on what had happened to their relationship a decade earlier. On 23 July 1947, he wrote, "I was extremely sorry to learn that your marriage hadn't worked out. That of course means that I made a serious mistake ten years ago. Thought I was doing the right thing at the time as I couldn't see you throwing yourself away on a 'dud' like me. We all learn many things the hard way, it seems." In a subsequent letter, written on 8 August 1947, Jenkins made his intentions perfectly clear when he wrote, "At the first opportunity I am again going to ask you to be my wife until death do us part. . . . As far as I am concerned you were the one and only." On 20 August, he wrote that he had a sabbatical leave the following year and that his "day dream" was for her to share it with him.[2]

Havreberg did not reject Jenkins's offer out rightly, but she began pursuing other opportunities with the foreign service. In July 1948, she accepted a position as a secretary with the newly established Economic Cooperation Administration in Paris, a United States State Department agency that administered the European Recovery Program, better known as the Marshall Plan, throughout western Europe. She resigned this position in the summer of 1950, returned to the United States, and married Tom Jenkins in Sioux Falls on 11 September 1950. The few surviving letters and personal papers from this period provide little information on her decision to marry Jenkins.[3]

For the first few years following her marriage, Havreberg held various secretarial positions in Minot. The couple had no children of their own, but they developed a close and loving relationship with her goddaughter and niece Sally Enstrom, with whom they shared many holidays and gatherings. This relationship took on an even deeper meaning following the death of Enstrom's mother and Havreberg's sister Lillian in 1955. Enstrom, who was only sixteen at the time of her mother's death, increasingly relied on her Aunt Marge for solace and "motherly" advice.

In 1954, after Tom Jenkins received his doctorate in education from the University of Oregon, he was appointed president of the State Normal and Industrial School in Ellendale, North Dakota. In 1959, he assumed the presidency of Mayville State Teachers College (now Mayville State University) in Mayville, North Dakota, a position he held until his retirement in 1974. The life of the wife of a college president was not easy for the adventuresome Havreberg, and in 1959, the couple briefly separated.[4]

In 1974, the Jenkinses retired to a cabin near Detroit Lakes, Minnesota, that they had purchased in the early 1960s. They enjoyed the outdoor life and became avid bird watchers. Marjorie Havreberg Steinbach Jenkins died on 29 November 1999 of colon cancer at the age of 85. Tom Jenkins, who was 91, died a few months later. In 1991, when reminiscing about their married life together, Havreberg wrote, "We have been lucky to have had so many good years and we're very grateful."[5]

Early in 1943, author and journalist Max Lerner wrote, "When the classic work on the history of women comes to be written, the biggest force for change in their lives will turn out to have been war."[6] Following the renewed interest in women's history during the 1960s and 1970s, United States historians began exploring this topic in great detail, providing a more nuanced interpretation of the war's influence. In 1982, writing in *The Home Front and Beyond*, Susan M. Hartmann concluded that, in the 1950s, "desire for the 'normalcy' denied by depression and war undermined the war's potential for challenging sex-role behavior and attitudes." Nonetheless, she also argued that the dramatic changes experienced by women in the 1940s "laid the preconditions for an awakened womanhood in the 1960s."[7] In her 1984 study, *Women at War with America,* D'Ann Campbell came to similar conclusions: "When, in 1945, American women . . . picked up life as usual, and benefitted from growing prosperity to devote time to their homes and families, they were not, in fact, returning to the world of their foremothers, but—consciously or not—reinterpreting it as a legacy for their daughters and granddaughters."[8]

Without question, Havreberg's experiences in Ankara served as a major force in her life. Although she eventually married her first romantic interest and lived a somewhat conventional life as the wife of a college president, she always cherished the memories of her assignment in Turkey, and she kept in touch with many of her Ankara colleagues long after she returned to the United States. Her passion for travel continued. She frequently visited friends and relatives in Arizona, Washington, D.C., and Minnesota, and she accompanied her niece on a grand tour of Europe in 1991. Havreberg, like so many other women of the World War II generation, returned to a world similar to that of her foremothers. But even in a traditional role, she would serve as a strong role model for young women, including her niece, who came of age in the post-World War II era.

NOTES

1. "Dear Jeff," 5 Mar. 1990, Marjorie Havreberg Steinbach Jenkins Papers, State Archives Collection, South Dakota State Historical Society, Pierre.

2. Jenkins's letters are in the Jenkins Papers.

3. Lillian Enstrom visited her sister in Paris in September–October 1949, but her letters to her husband and two children, which do survive, include little information about Havreberg and her life and work in Paris.

4. In an employment application to the National Academy of Sciences dated 27 May 1959, Havreberg states that she is married but separated. There are, however, a series of loving letters that Jenkins wrote to her during the spring and summer of 1959 that are included in the Jenkins Papers.

5. [Christmas letter, 1991], Jenkins Papers.

6. Lerner, *Public Journal: Marginal Notes on Wartime America* (New York: Viking Press, 1945), p. 19.

7. Hartmann, *The Home Front and Beyond: American Women in the 1940s* (Boston: Twayne Publishers, 1982), p. 216.

8. Campbell, *Women at War with America: Private Lives in a Patriotic Era* (Cambridge, Mass.: Harvard University Press, 1984), p. 238.

Remembering Aunt Marge

BY SALLY ENSTROM

My aunt and godmother, Marjorie Havreberg Steinbach Jenkins, was overseas during most of my early years. When she visited our home in Redfield, South Dakota, my older brother, Jack, and I were cautioned to be quiet in the morning because Aunt Marge was sleeping. Her large trunks sat in our basement, and I marveled at their immense size and all the compartments. My father sold suitcases at our family shoe store in Redfield, but not banged-up, oversized trunks with stickers all over them.

My earliest memory of Aunt Marge was when I was seven years old. It was the summer of 1946, and Aunt Marge had returned to Redfield following a two-year tour of duty in Ankara, Turkey, where she had served as the secretary to the United States military attaché. While in Ankara, she had taken a trip to the Middle East, and she gave me a beautiful mother-of-pearl Bible that she had purchased in Jerusalem. Her Polish friend Balo came with her to Redfield. What I remember most about Balo was his thick accent; it made him seem so different from anyone I had ever met.

The following year, Aunt Marge, who was then working for the United States military attaché in Ottawa, Canada, resigned her position in October and returned to Redfield to help my mother, Lillian, care for my grandmother, who died of colon cancer in December. It was a difficult time, and I remember the two of them quietly moving in and out of my grandmother's bedroom and always keeping the door closed.

From 1948 to 1950, Aunt Marge embarked on her final government assignment, working in Paris for the Economic Cooperation Administration, a division of the Department of State implementing the Marshall Plan. Since my father's shoe store was doing well, Mother suggested to Dad that perhaps she and her friend Eloise could travel to Europe to visit Marge. Dad agreed, even though it meant that he would be caring for Jack, my thirteen-year-old brother, and me, a ten year old, while also managing the shoe store. Mother wrote glowing letters to us during her two-month European tour in 1949. What a memorable time she and Eloise had, and what marvelous travel plans Aunt Marge arranged for them. When I finally was able to make a similar trip to Europe some twenty years later, I asked Aunt Marge to come to Minneapolis, where I lived, and help me organize and pack for the trip.

My fondest and most vivid memories of Aunt Marge are after she married Tom Jenkins in 1950. When I was about twelve years old, I spent part of my Christmas vacation with them in Minot, North Dakota, where Tom taught at Minot State Teacher's College. That was the infamous visit when we decided to see a movie. Because of our age differences, we each chose different movies. I was told to wait for Marge and Tom in the lobby of the theater after the show, but instead I walked back to their apartment on the college campus. When Aunt Marge and Tom couldn't find me, they called the police! They were so relieved when they finally discovered that, on my own, I had safely returned to their apartment.

A few years later, Tom received his doctoral degree, and in 1954, he became president of the State Normal and Industrial School in Ellendale, North Dakota. My mother died the following year, and Aunt Marge became an even more important part of my life. With the deaths of my brother in 1963 and my father in 1966, Aunt Marge was the person I turned to for support. She reached out to me in wonderful ways. I received a telephone call from her a year or so after Dad's death suggesting that we have Thanksgiving together at their cabin near Detroit Lakes, Minnesota. I thought it a splendid idea, and it was the beginning of many memorable holidays and vacations with them.

Tom did not enjoy traveling, but he did not object to his wife's need to see the world, and Aunt Marge and I enjoyed many adventures together. We visited Washington, D.C., traveled to Arizona to visit her sister Pat, and once we spent a few days with Marge's friend Sally Norbeck, the daughter of Senator Peter Norbeck, who also lived in Arizona. Later, when my Aunt Pat moved back to the Black Hills, Aunt Marge and I would drive out every summer for a visit, always stopping in Redfield on our way home. In late 1991, we even toured Europe together. This trip provided Aunt Marge with the opportunity to spend a day in Paris connecting with old friends still living in Europe. We traveled far and wide and lived in distant places, but South Dakota, the land and its people, remained a unifying and powerful force for both of us.

Aunt Marge especially enjoyed coming on the bus to visit me in Minneapolis. I would plan a few activities during the day, and in the evening, we would get together with my friends who soon became her friends, too. She was interested in everything and everybody, and she loved hearing about the experiences of others.

Summers at their cabin were especially happy times for Aunt Marge. Entertaining her many visitors, feeding the orioles, and gathering fresh flowers kept her busy. She developed a new way of preserving flowers and enjoyed making bookmarks and calendars for everyone. She even began memorizing things to keep her mind sharp. She memorized all the presidents in order, every country in the world with proper pronunciation, famous speeches, and much more.

I remember Aunt Marge for her intelligence and her warm and caring nature. She was always willing to listen and lend support. She loved meeting and being with people. Their stories became her stories. She had a sense of adventure, and she was always willing to try something new. A most remarkable woman, she was a mentor, confidant, and friend in all the best possible ways.

Appendix 1

Three versions of this typescript can be found in the Marjorie Havreberg Steinbach Jenkins Papers. It was evidently part of a larger manuscript about life and customs in the Turkish capital. The author is unknown, but references to Havreberg's roommate from Little Rock, Arkansas, suggest that Havreberg had a hand in its creation.

KARPITCH THE MAGNIFICENT
Şereful-mekân bilmekin

(The honor of a place depends upon its occupant.)
—*Arabic saying*

Perhaps the earliest of the tales told of this still-living, legendary personality is so true-seeming of both characters in the story that it may well have happened:

Trees were among the most cherished and protected articles in the young and barren capital of the Republic, Ankara, in the 1920s. To harm any one of those early, struggling acacias was reckoned nigh on treason by the beetling hustler, President Mustafa Kemal—later renamed Kemâl Atatürk. In those days Karpitch's City Restaurant provided a first-class haven of rest and refreshment for government officials, hard-driven deputies, and the few foreigners there in the growing town. The new buildings were just beginning to rise, streets were being planned and laid out and the stripling evergreens, with the endless rows of everlasting hardy acacias were coaxed into strength and maturity in that semi-parched climate. Three of these appear in this tale.

So well had these three trees succeeded in growing that, having been planted pessimistically close to the City Restaurant, they spread out their branches and fairly successfully formed a leafy barricade outside its door. Karpitch did not hesitate. Being Karpitch, he acted swiftly. He had two of the offending trees chopped down. It did not take long for Atatürk to notice this. He was furious and promptly summoned Karpitch. Being Atatürk, he put his question to Karpitch rather differently than would an ordinary man:

"Baba, why did you not cut down the third tree?"

But Karpitch—so goes the tale—was unabashed and quite ready with his reply:

"Excellence," said he, "it was necessary for me to leave something for you to hang me on."

A most unusual man, a magnanimous and magnificent man, a perfect host is Baba Karpitch; seeing all, neglecting none. He looks, as an American girl aptly put it, at one and the same time like a pirate chief and your favorite godfather. In his white silk jacket—you will never see him without it—great head and eagle's beak held high in air, swinging his long arms, he moves from table to table to see that his guests (all who enter are guests—for a mere customer there is no table space at Karpitch's) are well cared for. Eyes a-twinkle, the stoop-shouldered, beloved *restaurateur* adjusts a napkin here, calls for a second helping *gratis* there, then disappears for a moment into the pantry to emerge with a huge, unbelievable tangerine wrapped in green tissue paper, which he slyly lays on the table in front of a wide-eyed small boy, solemnly eating lunch with his mother, the wife of a Counselor of Embassy. He waits for no expression of thanks, but stalks up to a favored, pretty young girl to put his arms about her and soundly and unashamedly kiss her on the back of the neck. He notices something missing at the table where Prime Minister Şükrü Saracoğlu lunches each day with his military aide, his *chef de cabinet* and an occasional guest or two. With an air of enormous rage, Baba sends waiters and busboys scurrying in all directions to set things right. One imperious fling of his arm brings a nervous waiter racing up with the missing spoon or fork. When all is set to rights, Karpitch again goes off in the direction of the kitchen, this time to return with a large bowlful of costly Black Sea caviar, which he places with a courtly bow, hand on chest, on the Prime Minister's table, by way of apology for the waiter's sin of omission.

He came to Turkey, it is said, with the many thousands of White Russian refugees some twenty-five years ago, from Novorossiisk, where he had been an agent of oil companies, never a keeper of restaurants. His father, he says, "was a brigand, like me." But he is not informative about himself or his past and so one must accept—perhaps with some reserve—the version of one of his older waiters, who came to Turkey from Russia at about the same time. This man, the son of a

Crimean merchant, says that, as a boy, he remembers meeting Baba and the latter's father, also a merchant, in Moscow well over forty years ago. Karpitch, he says, is Armenian by race and his given name is Kevork (the Armenian equivalent of George) and his family name is Keçeciyan. If you wish to give the old man some gift in token of your appreciation of his kindness and generosity—it is done surprisingly often—do it on September 30th, his "name day," or on January 6th, Christmas Day in the Armenian Church calendar. His daughter-in-law and grand-daughter (he is a widower) dine regularly in the City Restaurant. The latter is a dark-eyed, lively little minx of about 5 or 6, whom her grand-daddy loves to fondle and call the "stupidest, ugliest little girl in all the world." She is nothing of the sort, of course, though Karpitch—with his unerring eye for a pretty face, should know. When his son died a few years ago, the life of the capital came almost to a standstill on the day of the funeral, attended by crowds of the great and near-great and ordinary folk. The young man's Christian grave is the only one in the Moslem cemetery.

He is the type, with the largeness of his mind and qualities carved into his features, and in spite of his shuffling, hobbling *restaurateur's* gait, which somehow dominates any gathering graced by his presence. Providing dinner and luncheon parties for Presidents and Prime Ministers, the *Shahinshah* of Iran, an Ambassador, or a visiting King is an everyday occurrence *chez* Karpitch. Somehow, if you glance at the distinguished gathering, it is always Karpitch who catches the eye—and not because of his silk jacket or because he is standing up.

The refugee from sovietized Russia worked first in Istanbul and later, it is believed at Atatürk's "suggestion," at Yalova. This is a small resort town built on the southern shore of the Sea of Marmara. It possesses natural hot springs, a sunny climate, one of Turkey's best hotels, and is only a few hours pleasant journey by ferry-boat from the Golden Horn bridge past the Prince's Isles. As a means of lightening the burden of life for those who were compelled to live in the new capital at Ankara, Atatürk recognized the need for a good eating place—and who better than Karpitch could run it? So to Ankara Baba went, there to find worldwide fame if not a great fortune. He is a boon and a blessing to all who dine and wine there now; how much more so he must have been in the days of republican Ankara's beginnings, to the *corps diploma-*

tique, for example, and to all *gourmets* and *gourmands* who may have had little fancy for their post in that distant and, in those days, primitive citadel high on the Anatolian plateau in the shadow of the crags of Hüseyin Gazi and Elma Dag.

Every facility is given Baba so that he may have, first, fish, fruit, and all manner of delicacies. It is whispered that he pays no taxes and that at such times as his excessive generosity in giving away costly wines and caviar with both hands has well-nigh emptied the Şehir Lokantasi (City Restaurant) cash-box, he has but to send to the municipal treasurer for more money and it is given him. It is not easy to establish the truth of such statements, but there is no doubt as to his incredible habits of *largesse*. You will see him—let us hope as the lucky recipient—dole out caviar, gobs and gobs of it, by the plateful at several hundred dollars the plate. All this at no cost to the fortunate guest, but merely to add to the enjoyment of his three dollar meal, with perhaps fifty dollars worth of imported champagne—also free—to make the meal even more pleasant. *Monsieur* Edouard, his *maitre d'hôtel*, despairingly told me that in 1945 the caviar bill alone, less such moneys as had been collected in payment for it, had cost the Restaurant some fifteen thousand dollars. Baba's philosophy, at the age of well past seventy, seems to be that money is no help beyond the grave. No wonder the favored girl from Little Rock, Arkansas, lazily stretched out her arms one day and murmured:

"Oh dear, I'm getting *so* tired of caviar."

There is the revealing story of the two British Embassy girls, close friends, who lunched and dined at Karpitch's almost every day for many months. There came a day when one of the girls came alone. Karpitch noticed this at once and asked after the other, but received only a smile in response. However, when the same girl continued to eat her meals alone, he insistently asked the same question and was told that the other girl had lost her position and couldn't afford to eat there anymore. For once, Baba's anger seemed real enough.

"You tell your friend she must eat here and only here," he said, "And tell her she must eat and drink anything she likes and bring her friends, too, if she likes. Tell her she is my guest and that I insist she must eat in my restaurant as long as she stays in Ankara. If she wants to pay me later, after she gets a job and some money, she can, but that isn't important. You tell her Karpitch is very angry and tell her what Karpitch says. Don't forget now."

The girl didn't forget, indeed, and the two friends showed up together for a dinner the next evening. They were served—free, of course—a banquet of Russian soup, lobster *en casserole á la Karpitch, Kievsky*, and *bombe surprise*, with Moselle and Rhine wines such as it is the lot of only the deep and full of pocket and of government representatives usually to enjoy. The girl got a good job soon after and settled her account happily with the *maitre d'hôtel*. Karpitch showed no interest in so trivial a detail as payment.

It is very pleasant indeed in the summer at Karpitch's when all—or nearly all—the tables are moved out into the quiet garden outside, with its adjacent public park. There is a stone dance-floor, a gypsy orchestra every evening and also at noon on Sundays, playing soft music while you dine and much too loud dance music, usually tunes you first heard years before, later at night. The lights hang from wires strung between the trees and, especially if you are lucky enough to secure a table in one of the low enclosures along the three outside, hedged-in sides, it is all very pleasant indeed. Here you may dine well, converse in a subdued, yet gay, atmosphere, dance if you wish and, if it amuses you, watch the cats and kittens—there always seem to be scores of them scampering about hunting for scraps of food or playing with each other. One such, a tiny, nondescript black-and-white kitten, took my fancy and (at the request of my table waiter) I took it home with me. Karpitch, who always knows everything that goes on in his place, inside or out, reproached me the next evening. My answer was that it meant nothing to him, except that some guest one evening who might happen to order a Karpitch *lièvre* (hare) would perhaps be out of luck. Baba shook his head reprovingly.

"Oh, so you think you are joking," said he. "Wait."

He shuffled off, swinging his arms, in the inimitable Karpitch manner, toward the inner recesses to reappear, sometime later, followed by two of his waiters, each bearing a silver salver. There was an unmistakable twinkle in Baba's eye and his tongue was in his cheek.

"Look!" he said, with a sweeping gesture.

We looked, my table companion and I.

On one of the salvers lay a long, red carcass, suspiciously feline. On the other was a long piece of fur, with legs, and—horrible sight!—a long tail. Unmistakably cat.

"So you think you are joking," said Karpitch, his shoulders shaking heavily as he waved the waiters back. He followed them still laughing silently to himself.

He has kept a book of autographs through the years, in which signatures and encomiums of the great and the not-great abound. They are in every conceivable language and many scripts and dialects; people from the four corners of the world have forgathered at this famous eating-place and many of them have written words of grateful praise in this book.

"A great Minister of the Interior," wrote an Englishman with much truth, if not first-rate wit. There are clippings from newspapers and magazines pasted into the book, as well as cartoons and sketches of the great man. One by the Turkish cartoonist Cemal Nadir Güler is excellent and depicts Baba truly to the life. The *National Geographic Magazine* is represented and you may read therein a typical story of Karpitch's courtesy to his guests when, on a hot summer day and when the windows refused to open, he stepped on a chair, wrapped a napkin around his fist and punched the offending window-panes out one by one. The book contains scores of signatures of interned American airmen, who during one phase of World War II were long a familiar sight in Karpitch's. He treated them all like young princes of the blood and they loved him. Baba—which is a term of affection for "father"—was the best of daddies to these stranded aviators whom the strange tides of the air war had blown into neutral Turkey and internment in accordance—generously interpreted by the Turks—with the rules of what is peculiarly termed international law.

It is noteworthy, perhaps, that operators of two other restaurants in Ankara at least are Karpitch graduates. Ohannes of the *Mutlu* was long a waiter in the City Restaurant, and Serge, a White Russian refugee, was for many years Karpitch's *maitre d'hôtel*; he now runs the expensive but pleasantly *intime_Sureyya Paviyonu* in Ankara's *Yenişehir* ("New City") below stairs in the building opposite *Kizilay* ("Red Crescent") headquarters near the unimposing American Embassy.

By dint of careful steering during Turkey's World War II period of neutrality, Karpitch managed to keep British, American, and other nationals on the one side from being seated too close to any table where Germans, Italians, Japanese, Bulgarians, or Rumanians were being fed. "Axis corner" usually contained both Japanese and German members of the diplomatic corps. "Incidents" were surprisingly few and were usually started by somebody singing or the orchestra playing songs or music offensive to one side or the other: "Tipperary," "The Siegfried Line," "Lily Marlene," and so on. When, on New Year's Eve, an enthusiastic guest grabbed the violinist's instrument and smashed it neatly over the bald head of a fellow-guest—who spent the next ten minutes seated on the floor, wearing an expression of hurt bewilderment and trying to untangle the mess from his shoulders—the cause was probably related less to the war than to the effects of a powerful concoction served at the bar called a "screwdriver," which consists of one-half Monopoly *votka* and one-half orange juice. The author was the first to sit in Axis corner after internment of Japanese in Turkey (the Germans had been taken care of months before); since there appeared to be no more Axis nationals to sit there, it seemed unnecessary to leave that perfectly good table empty. So, with my guests (some pro-ally Italians and others), I took the table. We were greeted by a round of applause from a British-occupied table nearby and cards of congratulations were sent us by the Polish Military Attaché and others. The battle of Karpitch's had at last been won.

Appendix 2. Karpiç Menu

Handwritten annotations: ORDINARY LUNCHEON MENU · TURKISH · FRENCH · City Restaurant KARPIC (KARPITCH)

Şehir Lokantası KARPİÇ

DO NOT PAY WITHOUT THE BILL

Faturasız tediye etmeyiniz. Ne pas payer sans facture.

NO BREAD without ration card

Karnesiz ekmek verilemez		Pas de pain sans carnet.
Taze Havyar	750 k.	Caviar frais
Siyah Havyar	500 k.	Caviar pressé
Salatalık	20 k.	Concombre.
Salata:Domates ve hiyar	75 k.	Salade:Tomates et concombres

16/8/1944   Öğle yemeği   200 k.   Saat 12 den 15 a kadar.

I

Patates ezme çorbası	Potage Parmentier
Et suyu soğuk ve sıcak	Consommé froid ou chaud
Tavuk ciğerli pilav	Pilav aux foies de volaille
Fasulyalı omlet	Omelette aux haricots
Kılıç ıskara	Espadon grillé
Tereyağlı bezelya	Petits pois au beurre
Patlican İmam bayildi	Aubergine Imam baildi

2

Bamyalı piliç	poussin sauté aux combeaux
Patlican karnıyerik	Aubergine farcie à la viande
Kuzu ciğeri tavası	Foie d'agneau sauté
Tavuk köfte Pojarsky	Boulettes de volaille Pojarsky
Salçalı biftek	Beefstacks braisé

3

Reçelli puding	Pudding à la confiture
Komposto:Elma; Erik	Compote: Pommes;Prunes
Dondurma:Vanilya; Kaysı	Glace: Vanille;Abricots
Meyve	Fruits
Kavun	Melon
Karpuz	Pasteque

Hususi yemekler   Plats speciaux (Special plates)

Çipura; Kefal	400	Dorade; Mulet
Jambon	350	Jambon
Antrekot	350	Entrecôte
İşnitzel	350	Schnitzel
Piliç	400	Poussin
Hindi	400	Dinde
Tavuk pirzolası	400	Cotelette de volaille
Kievsky	400	à la Kiev
Kuzu şişkebâb	400	Brochette d'agneau
Kuzu pirzolası	350	Cotelettes d'agneau

16/8/1944

196

Appendix 3. 22 October 1945 letter from South Dakota Congressman Karl E. Mundt

KARL MUNDT
1ST DIST. SOUTH DAKOTA

HOME ADDRESS:
MADISON, S. DAK.

COMMITTEES:
FOREIGN AFFAIRS
INDIAN AFFAIRS
SPECIAL COMMITTEE TO INVESTIGATE
UN-AMERICAN ACTIVITIES

Congress of the United States
House of Representatives
Washington, D. C.

October 22, 1945

Mr. and Mrs. Henry Havreberg
Redfield
South Dakota

Dear Friends:

While I was in Turkey on a mission for the House Foreign Affairs Committee from which I have recently returned, I had the pleasure of meeting your daughter, Marjorie, who is working in our American Embassy in Ankara.

Marjorie asked me to extend you her greetings and it is a pleasure for me to relay this message for her. I found your daughter feeling as fit as a fiddle and she is comfortably located in Ankara and doing a fine piece of work in the Embassy according to word given to me by her superiors in that office.

With best wishes and kindest personal regards, I am

Cordially yours,

Karl E. Mundt, M. C.

Appendix 4. Special Order No. 28 Ankara, Turkey, 18 April 1946

THE FOREIGN SERVICE
OF THE
UNITED STATES OF AMERICA
Office of the Military Attache

Ankara, Turkey
18 April 1946

SPECIAL ORDER)
)
NO. 28.......)

     1. .Under authority contained in MIS 2nd Ind to ltr MID 201 Steinbach, Marjorie H., dated 1 March 1946, Mrs. MARJORIE H. STEINBACH, Clerk, QMC, on duty this station, will proceed on or about 15 May 1946 from Ankara, Turkey to Washington, D.C. at Government expense for thirty (30) days TDY, and further orders. While on TDY in Washington, D.C. per diem of three dollars ($3.00) is authorized. TDN. Travel by water, commercial and/or military aircraft, and first class rail from point of entry into United States to Washington, D.C. is authorized. Per diem of seven dollars ($7.00) for all official travel performed outside the continental limits of the United States, and per diem of six dollars ($6.00) for all official travel within the United States is authorized. A baggage allowance of four hundred (400) pounds when traveling by rail and/or water, and a baggage allowance of sixty-five (65) pounds when traveling by commercial and/or military aircraft is authorized. 212/60425 88-135 P 432-02, 03, 07, 08.

                                    /s/ J.E. Harriman
                                    J.E. HARRIMAN
                                    Colonel, GSC
                                    Military Attache

OFFICIAL:
Military Attache
Embassy of the United States of America
Turkey

A Certified true copy

SAMUEL J. OFFIE
Capt, TC
Asst T Comdr, USAT W.A. Holbrook

Appendix 5. Commendation Letter

OFFICE OF THE MILITARY ATTACHE

Ankara, Turkey
15 July 1946
15 May 1946?

SUBJECT: Commendation to Mrs. Marjorie Steinbach

TO   : Clerk, Quartermaster Corps
          The Pentagon
          Washington, D.C.

   1. It is desired to commend Mrs. Marjorie Steinbach, Clerk, Quartermaster Corps, who has left recently after a two-year tour of duty in the Office of the Military Attache, Ankara, Turkey.

   2. Mrs. Steinbach is commended for her exemplary performance of duty as secretary in the Office of the Military Attache, in which assignment her services were characterized by hard work, efficiency, and devotion to duty.

   3. Apart from her high technical standards it is a pleasure to mention Mrs. Steinbach's conscientious and cheerful attitude, and her never-failing willingness to help others and to place service ahead of self.

                        J. E. HARRIMAN
                        Colonel, GSC

Index

48, 53, 54, 56, 59, 60–62; postwar
visits with, 186; shopping with, 53;
social events with, 32–33, 35–38, 40,
43–46, 48, 50–52, 57–60; and ward-
robe, 53, 57, 120
Norbeck family, residence with, 6, 54,
56
Nye, Gerald K., 65n8

One World (Willkie), 89, 90
Örge, Binbaşi, 143
Ottowa, Canada, Havreberg in, 179–80,
185

Packer, Earl L. and Mrs., 100, 155
Palestine, Havreberg's travel in, 17,
134–35
Paris: Havreberg in, 180, 185–87; libera-
tion of, 18
Park Palas (hotel), 15, 98–101, 105
Peasants, Turkish, 122–23
Penna's (restaurant), 132
Pierre, S.Dak., Havreberg in, 6, 64
Pillet, Frederick A., 140
Polish Embassy, 109–10, 118, 138
Polish government-in-exile, representa-
tives in Turkey, 14–15, 19–20, 106,
122, 150, 175n30
Politics, Havreberg and 4–5, 18, 22, 33
Porter, Quincy, 40
Pyramids of Egypt, 9, 97, 104, 115

Raki (beverage), 116
Redfield, S.Dak., 1–2, 6, 179, 180, 185
Reed, Jim, 57–58
Rizan, Cadri, 165
Romantic life, of Havreberg: in Ankara,
14–15, 18, 106–8, 135, 137–38; mar-
riages, 6, 18, 24n1, 25n18, 64, 175n28,
180–81, 186; in Redfield, 2–3; in

Washington D.C., 4, 36, 47–48, 49–
50, 51–52, 53, 55, 56, 59–60, 61–62.
See also Balinski, Antoni
Roosevelt, Franklin D., 2, 18–19, 124,
140
Ross, Peter V., 42
Ross, William F., 168
Rudnicki, Jan, 15, 104–5
Rudowski, Janek, 106, 107, 109–10, 150

Sandburg, Carl, 47
Sand flies, 99, 105, 112, 113, 123–24
Saracoğlu, Sükrü, 20, 139, 159, 175n26,
190
Saturday Evening Post, 11, 12, 99, 105
Seager, Cedric, 136
Seager, Walter Ewart, 15, 124, 130, 132,
133, 136, 155, 156, 158, 161, 168
Serge's (restaurant), 118, 120, 122, 124,
128, 129, 137, 142, 143, 155, 159
Shepheard's Hotel, 9, 21, 26n26, 104,
172, 173n10
Short, Jeffrey, 15, 101, 108, 110, 124, 126,
130, 132, 137, 168, 179
Sipp, Virginia, 123, 139, 142, 144, 169
Skinner, Cornelia Otis, 5
Soil Conservation and Domestic Allot-
ment Act of 1936, 65n7
Sompfin, Glenn, 52
South Dakota Society, 51, 52, 53
State Department, Havreberg's employ-
ment in, 7, 87, 180
Staten Island Ferry, 46
Stavangerfiord (ship), 46
Steinbach, Paul, 6, 18, 24n1, 25n18, 64,
119, 175n28
Steinhardt, Dulci Ann, 121, 174n17
Steinhardt, Laurence A., 12, 14, 124–26,
128, 132, 136, 174n17, 175n25
Sterling (friend), 45, 46